CARS OF THE STATE POLICE

AND

HIGHWAY PATROL

BY MONTY McCORD

Published by

 **krause publications**

700 E. State Street • Iola, WI 54990-0001

Please call or write for our free catalog of automotive publications. Our toll-free number
to place an order or obtain a free catalog is 800-258-0929 or please use our regular
business telephone 715-445-2214 for editorial comment
and further information.

Library of Congress Catalog Number: 94-74170
ISBN: 0-87341-319-9
Printed in the United States of America

CONTENTS

ACKNOWLEDGEMENTS

I would like to gratefully acknowledge the individuals and law enforcement agencies who provided information and photographs in order to make this project a success.

A special thanks goes to Captain Bryan J. Tuma, Sergeant Mike Phinney, and Trooper Andy Allen of Troop C, Nebraska State Patrol.

My deepest appreciation goes to Kay Nitz for her assistance in preparing the manuscript.

My sincere thanks goes to the following:

Judy Ames
John Antonelli
Jack Attig, Jr.
James Baldwin
Jim Benjaminson
Robert Clope
Jim Donohoe
Harold Fay
Jack Fellenzer
Scott Filis
Ken Gipson
Jon Goldin
Mark Grechniw
Francis Harr
Joe Hill
Brian Jackson
Earl Jensen
Terry Jessee
G.M. Jones
Darryl Lindsay
Mike Martin
Michael Morelli
Thomas Parkinson
James Post
Greg Reynolds
Anthony Romano
Ronald Rysavy
Clifford Schneider
Ned Schwartz
John Shagath
Mark Shinost
Richard L. Story, Sr.
Hugh E. Thomas, Jr.

Jay Weinstein
LTC. Richard Williams, U. S. A.
Rod Williams
John Yeaw
North Dakota State Historical Society
Alabama State Troopers
Alaska State Troopers
Arizona Highway Patrol
Arkansas State Police
California Highway Patrol
Colorado State Patrol
Connecticut State Police
Delaware State Police
Florida Highway Patrol
Georgia State Patrol
Idaho State Police
Illinois State Police
Indiana State Police
Iowa State Patrol
Kansas Highway Patrol
Kentucky State Police
Louisiana State Police
Maine State Police
Maryland State Police
Massachusetts State Police
Michigan State Police
Minnesota State Patrol
Mississippi Highway Safety Patrol

Missouri State Highway Patrol
Montana Highway Patrol
Nebraska State Patrol
Nevada Highway Patrol
New Hampshire State Police
New Jersey State Police
New Mexico State Police
New York State Police
North Carolina Highway Patrol
North Dakota State Patrol
Ohio State Highway Patrol
Oklahoma Highway Patrol
Oregon State Police
Pennsylvania State Police
Rhode Island State Police
South Carolina Highway Patrol
South Dakota Highway Patrol
Tennessee Highway Patrol
Texas Highway Patrol
Utah Highway Patrol
Vermont State Police
Virginia State Police
Washington State Patrol
West Virginia State Police
Wisconsin State Patrol
Wyoming Highway Patrol

I apologize to any contributor I may have omitted.

Anyone interested in the hobby of police vehicles: full size, miniatures, photographs, or equipment, should contact:

James Post
Police Car Owners of America
Route 6, Box 112
Eureka Springs, Arkansas 72632

Police Collectors News
Rural Route One, Box 14
Baldwin, Wisconsin 54002

ABOUT THE AUTHOR

The author is currently a lieutenant with the Hastings, Nebraska, Police Department. He began his law enforcement career in 1974 as an Adams County Deputy Sheriff. He served as a Phelps County Deputy Sheriff before joining the Hastings Police in 1978.

Upon entering law enforcement, a hobby of collecting police memorabilia began. An avid law enforcement historian, McCord published a book in 1982 on his department's history. He has written several articles for Police Collectors News on various facets of the hobby. His historical law enforcement articles have appeared in The Nebraska Police Officer and The Texas State Peace Officers Journal. He continues building a collection of police insignia for which he has received "best display" awards at collectors' conventions in Kansas City, Missouri; Denver, Colorado; and Torrington, Wyoming. A lifelong interest in cars underwent a slight transition resulting in a certain fondness for police vehicles. His current project car (shown above) is a 1962 Plymouth Savoy restored as a cruiser of the period. The car is driven to out-of-state Police Car Owners Of America conventions as well as cruise nights at local drive-ins. McCord collects miniature police cars as well as photographs for future book projects.

In 1991 his book, Police Cars-A Photographic History was published by Krause Publications. The book was featured in AutoWeek magazine. In his "spare time," McCord operates a part-time police insignia business in which he designs and sells badges and patches to many different agencies.

In 1993 he graduated from the 174th session of the FBI National Academy in Quantico, Va. He is a member of the Police Car Owners Of America, the FBI National Academy Associates, the Police Officers Association Of Nebraska, the Nebraska State Historical Society, the Adams County Neb. Historical Society, the Wyoming State Historical Society, the National Association For Outlaw-Lawman History and the Western Outlaw-Lawman History Association.

INTRODUCTION

State police, state patrol, or highway patrol refers to the agency responsible for state-wide traffic law enforcement and frequently includes criminal investigation duties for that state. I've attempted to present as accurately as possible the patrol cars used by all forty-nine state police and highway patrol agencies in the United States. City and county agencies provide law enforcement in Hawaii, which does not have a state police force. Each chapter begins with a brief history of the department's evolution. The latest patrol cars are shown first in the chapter and progress backward chronologically. Many of the door emblems and license plates, new and old, are shown. Many of the departments changed organizationally resulting in different names, door emblems, and insignia. This is a way to approximate time periods of photos.

A GLANCE AT STATE POLICE ORIGINS

American state police agencies began to take shape toward the end of the nineteenth century. These agencies were organized for a variety of reasons ranging from enforcement of specific laws to providing law enforcement for areas without local police. Lawmakers often met with resistance when offering legislative bills to create state police agencies as it was feared that the state would override local authority. In spite of opposition, by the 1920s, the automobile provided one of the major reasons the state police came into existence. The automobile had changed the lives of people everywhere. Law abiding citizens could travel further and more often. As more and more vehicles took to the road, traffic laws were passed to regulate their operation and to promote safety. Traffic accidents claimed many lives as shown in Iowa from the years 1926 to 1930 at which time traffic related deaths rose from three hundred-twelve to over six hundred. The job of enforcing traffic safety regulations became a necessity.

The following is a look at how a few state police agencies got their start.

Pennsylvania was primarily an agricultural area until the 1900s when it evolved into a major industrial state. Industry caused an influx of population. Violent disputes between labor and management factions became so common that the local constables and sheriffs were unable to handle the problems. Management circles convinced the Commonwealth to create the infamous Coal and Iron Police, which were hired guns to enforce the will of the industrialists. The Great Anthracite Strike in 1902 almost turned seven Pennsylvania counties into a war zone. The fiasco ended only after President Theodore Roosevelt interceded. This strike made it evident that an officially appointed state police force was necessary.

A mounted officer of the Pennsylvania State Police, known as "Black Hussars." This group of two hundred mounted troopers was credited with breaking up a 1910 strike of 6,000 members of the Philadelphia Rapid Transit District Company.

On May 5, 1905, Senate Bill 278 was signed into law creating the Pennsylvania State Police. Organized labor was concerned that the state police would be nothing but a private army. Their influence was able to restrict the number of officers to less than two hundred-fifty. These men, mounted on horses, were responsible for patrolling 45,000 square miles of the state! By 1919, the state police established motorcycle patrols to handle the growing number of motorists. The new agency built a reputation for being effective and fair. Seventy motorcycles were obtained in 1920 with fourteen being assigned to each of the five troop areas. Patrol zones were established and citizens along the patrol route who owned telephones were given steel discs or flags that were hung out to tell the area trooper when to call his station.

A state highway patrol was created by legislature in 1923 with the Department of Highways to enforce the state's motor vehicle laws. At that time, the state police installed the first statewide police radio telegraph system in the United States. This system was used until 1947.

In 1937 a legislative act combined the Pennsylvania State Police with the Highway Patrol to form the Pennsylvania Motor Police. A last reorganization came in 1943 and the agency was named the Pennsylvania State Police.

The state of Iowa conducted a one month experiment in 1933 in which fifteen unarmed motor vehicle inspectors dressed in civilian attire took part. Their job was to assist motorists who were stranded and warn drivers of traffic violations. This experiment won favorable comment with one exception. Some people were afraid of being pulled over by plain-clothed officers. The fifteen inspectors were required to purchase their own uniforms and were given first aid training before returning to the field.

Iowa troopers issuing a traffic ticket circa 1935.

After vigorous lobbying, a bill creating the Iowa Highway Patrol was passed. An amendment to the bill required that no more than sixty percent of the fifty-three new patrolmen could belong to one political party. Qualifications of the original fifty patrolmen included: a minimum age of 25, a minimum height of five feet-ten inches, must be Iowa resident, and must be of "good moral character." After a seven week training session, the original patrolmen were assigned to new 1935 Ford sedans and Indian motorcycles. They worked twelve hour shifts, six days a week, with no weekends or holidays off. They were on twenty-four hour call, but received no overtime pay. Vehicles had radio receivers only with broadcasts from headquarters put out at certain times of the day. The first two-way radios were installed in Iowa Highway Patrol cars in 1943.

Perhaps the justification for a state patrol was stated best by Missouri Governor Arthur M. Hyde when he addressed the General Assembly in 1923: "The best machinery for law enforcement by state authority yet devised is a state police force. Such a police force can be trained. It is not hampered by county line. It can police and protect the state highways. Its sole reason for existence would then be to enforce the law equally and equitably in every county of the state, and without fear or favor to protect every citizen in the exercise of his right to life, liberty, and property."

The push for a highway patrol continued into the late 1920s. Some people believed that this type of organization needed full police powers, with others holding that only traffic enforcement powers were necessary. In 1929 gangsters moved in and out of the state, increasing organized crime activities. Finally, in 1931, a bill passed that formed the Missouri State Highway Patrol. Section 13 of the Senate Bill stated that, "The members of the patrol shall have the powers now or hereafter vested by law in peace officers except the serving or execution of civil process. The members of the patrol shall have authority to arrest without writ, rule, order, or process any person detected by him in the act of violating any law of the state." The new agency was allowed to hire one hundred-fifteen patrolmen at a yearly salary of not more than $1,800. Requirements to be hired included: applicant had to be at least 24 years old, must not have been convicted of any offense, had to be of good character, had to be a U.S. citizen, had to be able to read and write the English language, and had to pass a mental and physical examination. In addition, one half of the applicants had to be members of the political party casting the highest number of votes for governor in the last state election. Of 5,000 applicants, only fifty-five men were chosen to be the first Missouri State Patrolmen because funding for the entire one hundred-fifteen men failed to be appropriated. The uniforms, which were paid for by the patrolmen, were modelled after those worn by the New Jersey State Police. The only firearm issued to them was a .38 caliber Smith & Wesson revolver at a cost of $19.25 each.

The following vehicles were issued to the new patrolmen: thirty-six 1931 Model A Ford roadsters, one Model A sedan, one Plymouth sedan, one Oldsmobile, one Buick, three Chevrolet sedans and seventeen motorcycles including Harley-Davidsons, Indians, and Hendersons. The Ford roadsters cost $413.18 each and were equipped with two Klaxon horns, a spotlight, a fire extinguisher, a first aid kit, and red electric sign which read "Patrol" that was mounted on the right side of the windshield. This was the only marking the cars had. They had no siren as eastern state police agencies found that sirens terrified the citizens, sometimes causing accidents.

The people of Georgia were experiencing similar problems with accidents and mobility of criminals in the early 1930s due to increased motor travel. In 1931, the first bill was introduced in an attempt to create a state highway patrol. It was not until March of 1937, however, that Act 220 was signed into law. This act created the Georgia Department of Public Safety, which consisted of three divisions: the uniformed Georgia State Patrol, criminal investigation division, and the drivers licensing division. Eighty men became the first Georgia State Troopers. They were paid $1,200 per year.

One of the original thirty-six Model A Ford roadsters of the Missouri State Highway Patrol. Note the electric "PATROL" sign on the windshield.

Their first patrol cars were gun-metal colored 1937 Fords with the words "GEORGIA STATE PATROL" in orange letters painted on the sides of the hoods. These cars, which cost the state $710 each, featured bulletproof windshields.

The state of Washington, realizing the necessity of traffic regulation enforcement, created the Highway Patrol in 1921. The first six patrolmen rode Harley-Davidson and Indian motorcycles. Their police powers were limited to enforcement of traffic laws on the state highways. Legislature did not allow the patrolmen to wear uniforms until 1924. In the early years positions with the patrol were politically influenced as illustrated by the actions of Chief William Cole in 1925. Soon after taking command he reduced the force of patrolmen from thirty to seven and began recruiting men of his choice.

By the end of 1927, the state approved a force of fifty-seven patrolmen. Most of these men had to use their own cars for patrol. That year the highway patrol purchased a new Ford panel truck that was used as a paddy wagon.

The agency was given full police powers and the name was changed to the Washington State Patrol in 1933. That year the first radio was installed on a motorcycle. The radio operated on a Portland frequency. Motorcycles were phased out in the 1930s and replaced by panel delivery type vehicles. By 1937, one hundred-six officers were employed at a salary of $125 monthly.

Oklahoma reported a substantial increase in the number of motor vehicles operating in the state. About five hundred traffic deaths a year were recorded during the mid-1920s. In 1929 there were 600,000 vehicles using the roads. The state did not have the capabilities to enforce traffic regulations. Another problem was the high mobility of the lawless element. Many criminals, including the infamous "Pretty Boy" Floyd and Bonnie and Clyde, plagued the Oklahoma lawmen. Many prominent citizens campaigned for the organization of a state police agency. The general population was suspicious of a central state authority so it was not until 1935 that the state agency got its start. That year legislature authorized the creation of a twelve man state police force as part of the Stolen Car Division of the Oklahoma Tax Commission. The six cars allotted to these men made it impossible for them to be effective across the entire state.

This 1922 photo shows one of the original Washington state patrolman on an Indian motorcycle. Notice he is not wearing a uniform. Patrolmen in Washington were not allowed to wear uniforms until 1924.

Politics hampered the growth of the force with the opposition being afraid Governor Murray would have a "personal" police force. Murray's successor, Ernest Marland, convinced the legislature to create the Oklahoma Department of Public Safety in 1937. He convinced politicians by including civilian employees in the new agency. The Highway Patrol was that department's law enforcement arm.

Out of five hundred applicants, one hundred-forty were chosen to attend the first patrol training academy. At the time the salary of $150 per month was enticing. The first patrol cars were 1937 Ford two-door sedans painted black with white sides. The doors displayed an emblem in the shape of Oklahoma with the words "OKLAHOMA HIGHWAY PATROL." Some of the one hundred-five graduating patrolmen were part of "The Flying Squadron." These officers rode Indian motorcycles twelve to fourteen hours a day all year long, rain or shine!

In 1927, the Nebraska legislature created the office of State Sheriff for the purpose of enforcing criminal laws across the state. Unfortunately, this office was not equipped to deal effectively with the crime rate or the growing problems with traffic control. As early as 1925, there was talk of a need for an agency to regulate motor vehicle travel. Governor McMullen stated that a need for promotion of traffic safety and to penalize inept and careless drivers was evident. Traffic enforcement duties were carried out by local and county officials for the most part.

A legislative bill passed in 1937 created the division of Highway Safety and Patrol, which was part of the Department of Roads and Irrigation. Over 3,500 men applied for patrolmen positions with the Nebraska Safety Patrol. The sixty-four recruits that attended the first training camp were on an average 30 years of age and were six feet tall. In November of 1937, forty-four men swore an oath and became Nebraska's first state troopers. Wages for the new patrolmen were $100 per month during a probationary period with a $25 raise afterward. They worked twelve hour shifts, six days a week. No holidays or weekends off were allowed. The first patrol vehicles consisted of 1937 Ford two-door sedans and Indian motorcycles.

The Nebraska Safety Patrol received full police powers in 1941 when the Patrol absorbed the office of State Sheriff. All officers of the Safety Patrol were commissioned as Deputy State Sheriffs.

Those early days of road patrol were challenging. The cars had no police radios so a system was set up where selected service stations and roadside cafes would hang out a red pennant that would direct the patrolman to contact his supervisor for assignments. Sometimes a civilian radio station was used to broadcast emergency messages.

Vermont was one of the last states in the country to form a state police agency. The Vermont Legislature first considered the forming of such an agency in 1935. For some reason a state police bill was defeated in 1937 even after the legislature was presented with a study that showed an obvious need for the agency.

Unfortunately, the disappearance of a college student in 1947 was by and large responsible for a bill passing that created the Vermont State Police. The citizenry was outraged at the failure of local law enforcement to find any trace of the student who had been hiking. The State Police began operations with fifty-seven patrolmen. These men worked ninety hours per week with one night off. They were allowed one day off every two weeks, but could have no vacations during the summer and had no weekends or holidays off. Wages figured out to be about $48 a week.

Faced with an image to build in the beginning, state police agencies have come a long way. They started with minimal equipment and training and vehicles that were not designed to meet the challenges of police work. As their duties changed

A Nebraska patrolman posed in 1939 with his unit. This car shows the original door emblem of the Nebraska Safety Patrol, which includes the state capitol building in its design.

throughout the years, so did their training and equipment. With the arrival of the "police package" in the 1950s, patrol cars were more capable of handling law enforcement duties. Vehicle technology has constantly evolved. Modern cars provide safe, effective, and comfortable transportation for today's trooper.

ALABAMA STATE TROOPERS

The Alabama Highway Patrol originated in 1935. The agency was reorganized into the Department of Public Safety in 1939 with the Highway Patrol a division of the new D.P.S. In 1963, the Highway Patrol became the Alabama State Troopers.

This door emblem was used in the 1940s

The current door emblem of the Alabama State Troopers.

Alabama is one of many states to incorporate air units as support for the road troopers.

A 1991 Chevrolet Caprice of the Alabama State Troopers.

This mid-1970s Ford still uses the single blue rotator on the roof.

An Alabama trooper poses with his gray Dodge St. Regis.

This Ford Crown Victoria uses dash and grille lights instead of a roof unit.

This Mustang features a scaled-down door emblem along with the STATE TROOPER designation.

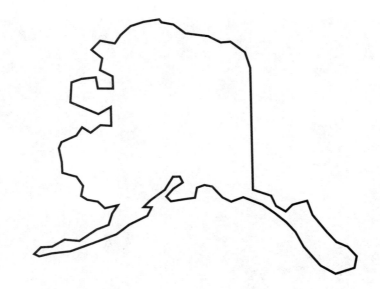

ALASKA STATE

TROOPERS

The Alaska Highway Patrol was organized in 1941. The name was changed to Alaska Territorial Police in 1953 when criminal investigations were added to traffic enforcement duties. The Department of Public Safety was created in 1959 with the Alaska State Police as one of its divisions. The current name, Alaska State Troopers, was adopted in 1967.

Door emblems used through the years in Alaska.

The current door emblem of the Alaska State Troopers.

This Alaska trooper poses with his new Chevy.

A Dodge Ramcharger in its "natural" habitat.

A Plymouth Gran Fury used by Alaska troopers.

Cruisers of the Alaska State Troopers are white with a black hood.

By 1959 the Alaska Territorial Police had changed to Alaska State Police. Shown here is a 1959 Ford.

A trooper poses with his 1957 Ford Ranch Wagon. Alaska had a "Territorial Police" at this time.

A 1956 Ford of the Alaska Territorial Police.

A 1954 Ford wearing Territorial Police markings.

This 1954 Ford Courier Sedan Delivery sold new for $1,590.

This photo was taken in 1953 as the Territorial Police sign would indicate. Buick patrol cars still carry "Highway Patrol" markings.

Hudson Hornets at the Alaska Highway Patrol office in Fairbanks.

This photo illustrates the new and old. A modern vehicle with Alaska troopers in their current uniform and a 1950s Hudson with a trooper in a uniform of that period.

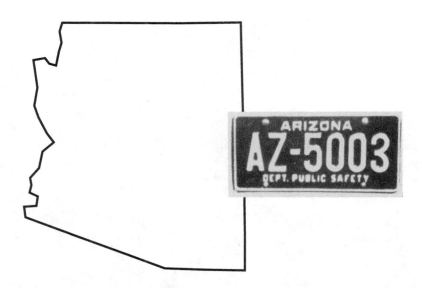

ARIZONA HIGHWAY PATROL

The Arizona Highway Department added a new division in 1931, the Arizona Highway Patrol. In 1969, the Arizona Department of Public Safety was organized. It is comprised of the Highway Patrol and four other state departments.

This door emblem is much like the current style with the exception of the wording. The new style reads Department of Public Safety Arizona.

This Lincoln Town Car is used as a test vehicle for the Ford Motor Company. That's called "cruising in style"!

A Ford Crown Victoria of the Arizona Highway Patrol.

Another "stylish" cruiser, the Ford Thunderbird of the Arizona Highway Patrol.

The 1990-91 Ford Taurus police package was discernable by the slots between the headlights.

A 1988 Ford Mustang. The venerable horse is still used in Arizona!

This four-wheel-drive Chevy pickup is equipped with a winch.

This mid-1980s Crown Victoria utilizes yellow lights mounted on the push bar.

A Plymouth Trailduster 4x4!

This slick Ford Probe wears Arizona Department of Public Safety "stars."

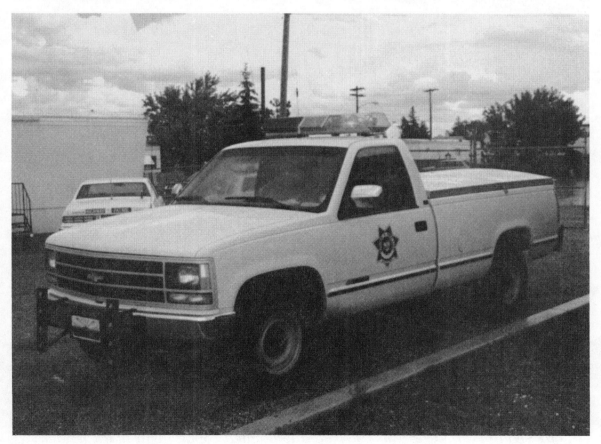

A Chevy pickup used for commercial vehicle enforcement.

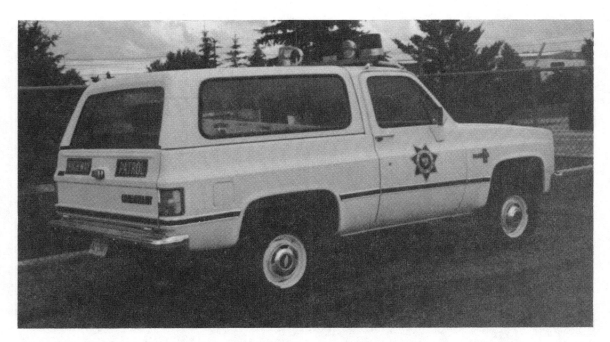

This Chevy Blazer carries rescue equipment.

A 1968 Chevrolet of the Arizona Highway Patrol poses with a restored 1931 Model A Ford Sedan Patrol Car. The 1931 Ford is painted copper with black fenders as they were when first used by the A.H.P. (Photo courtesy Arizona D.P.S.)

ARKANSAS STATE POLICE

The Arkansas State Police was formed in 1937. The State Police was made a part of the newly formed Arkansas Department of Public Safety in 1971.

The current door emblem of the Arkansas State Police.

This Chevy Caprice is outfitted with an older style blue strobe light bar.

A currently used Chevrolet Caprice of the Arkansas State Police.

This Chevy Caprice models the current markings of the Arkansas State Police.

This Chevrolet, a 1972 model, is unmistakably blue and white.

A trooper poses with his 1966 Ford.

This 1953 Ford has had some "off road" use.

CALIFORNIA HIGHWAY PATROL

The California Highway Patrol was formed in 1929. It became a division of the California Department of Motor Vehicles in 1931. From 1948 to the present, the California Highway Patrol has been a separate department.

The current door emblem of the California Highway Patrol.

This shiny Camaro is outfitted with a Vision light bar.

The Highway Patrol was a part of the California Department of Motor Vehicles from 1931 to 1948. This door emblem was used until 1946.

A radically different Vision light bar sits atop this new Crown Victoria.

This Caprice has a non-traditional "all white" paint job.

This Caprice is outfitted with a strobe light bar.

Ford Crown Victorias lined up on the grounds of the California Highway Patrol Academy.

This all white Crown Victoria is a K-9 unit.

A modern Mustang at the CHP Academy.

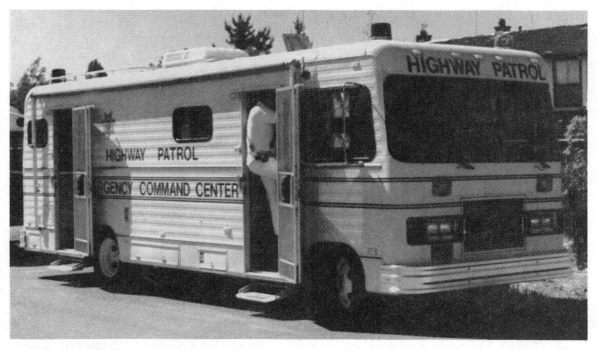

A Barth emergency command center.

Believe it or not, this Toyota Camry was tested for patrol use.

A shiny Chevrolet Suburban!

The Chevy Malibu was tested in the early 1980s by some departments including the CHP.

This Dodge Diplomat displays a different door emblem. The emblem was used on units under a special federal program, the enforcement of the 55 mph speed limit.

The CHP has been a test bed of prototype cruisers for years. This Chevy Celebrity was one such car tested.

A Chevy van equipped for accident investigation.

A 4x4 Jeep Cherokee being prepared for service.

A Ford four-door pickup in the service of the CHP.

This four-wheel-drive Dodge Ramcharger is used in the mountainous areas of California.

This pickup, a standard Dodge, is a mobile scale and truck inspection unit.

A trooper stopped to fuel this four-wheel-drive AMC Eagle.

When you need to get there fast ...

The "horse" that started a permanent career in law enforcement, a 1982 Mustang.

This early 1980s Mustang was unusual in that it was the only "fastback" model used.

One of twelve 1979 Chevrolet Camaros tested by the CHP.

One of the cars tested in 1979 by the California Highway Patrol were these Plymouth Volare station wagons.

A 1975 Dodge equipped with a 440 cubic inch V-8 engine.

A 1972 Dodge of the California Highway Patrol.

The CHP's talking Volkswagen, Otto, is a successful community relations tool.

In the early 1970s, the CHP used a limited number of roof mounted light bars as pictured on this 1972 Dodge.

A 1971 Dodge.

A 1970 Mercury.

A traffic officer strikes a pose with his 1964 Dodge.

California Highway Patrolmen test driving two 1960 models, a Dodge and a Pontiac.

A beautiful 1959 Dodge!

Three roof lights, two front, one rear, adorn this 1952 Ford.

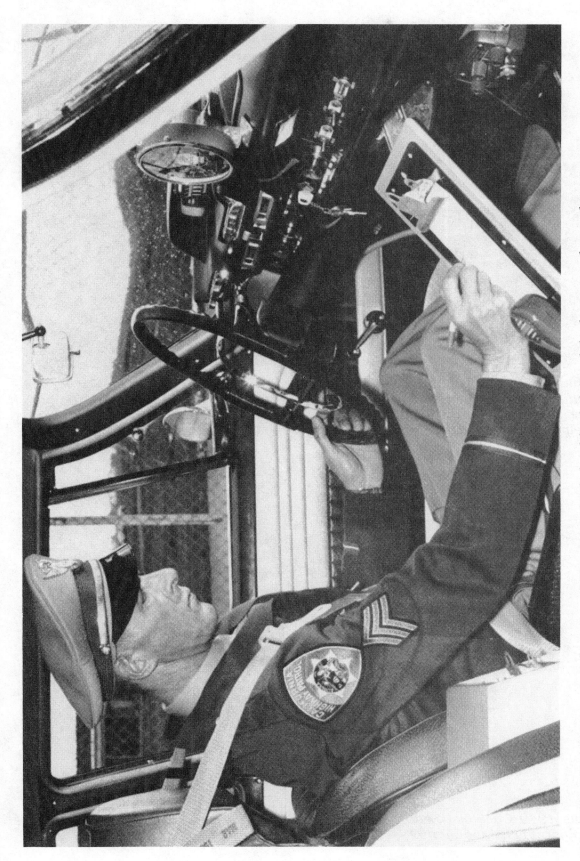

An interesting interior shot from the 1950s. Note dual shoulder belts and dash mounted speedometer.

The 1955 Buick Century two-door sedans were built only for the California Highway Patrol. The Special body was used, but from the firewall forward, the patrol car was a Century. Using this body for patrol cars had another advantage. It helped Buick come in as the low bidder for the CHP contract.

This 1949 Chevrolet Sedan Delivery served as a technical research unit for the California Highway Patrol.

This 1946 Buick appears ready for patrol.

This cruiser lineup consists of (left to right): a 1937 Buick, a 1937 Studebaker, and a 1936 Buick.

Obviously not sunny "Southern" California! This Model A Ford is lettered simply "California Highway Patrol" on its doors.

COLORADO STATE PATROL

The Colorado State Highway Courtesy Patrol was organized in 1935. Because of the excessive length of the name, it was shortened to Colorado State Patrol in 1945.

The current door emblem of the Colorado State Patrol resembles the trooper's hat badge.

This is a close facsimile of the door emblem used from 1945 to 1961. The actual emblem read "COLORADO STATE HIGHWAY" above the seal, and "PATROL" underneath.

The original door marking, used from 1937 to 1945.

The new look of the 1994 Camaro, this one in service in Colorado.

A Camaro RS, complete with scenic background.

It's not surprising to see four-wheel-drive vehicles in Colorado. Shown are a GMC Sierra (above) and a Dodge Ramcharger (below).

This pair of Plymouth Gran Furies sport different light bars.

The "business end" of a C.S.P. Mustang.

This patrolman poses with his Plymouth on an interstate overpass.

A 1974 Plymouth Fury I outside of a headquarters building.

A 1973 Plymouth Fury I outside of a headquarters building.

A 1966 Plymouth with roof mounted siren and light.

Colorado state patrolmen having a roadside discussion. The cruiser is a 1956 Ford.

This black and white 1946 Ford features a red grille light and spotlight on the windshield post.

Colorado Courtesy Patrol unit #152 with trailer.

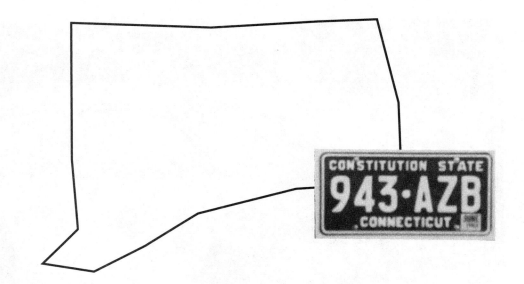

CONNECTICUT STATE POLICE

Created in 1903, the Connecticut State Police is one of the oldest state police agencies in the United States.

This Crown Victoria, a 1992 model, is light brown.

These Fords, one dark blue and the other gray, illustrate the various colors used by the Connecticut State Patrol.

A dark blue 1986 Ford Crown Victoria.

An emergency services prisoner transport van.

A 1975 Plymouth Gran Fury. Markings on Connecticut State Police cars are traditionally mounted on the removable light bar. The state police officers are encouraged to use their cars while off duty, enabling them to respond quickly to an emergency.

One of twenty-six Cadillac ambulances built by the Flxible Company in 1942. This one, used by the Connecticut State Police, was equipped with dual warning lights built into the roof and fender skirts. It had small signs in the side windows that read "CONN. STATE POLICE" in addition to lettering on the door.

DELAWARE STATE POLICE

The Delaware State Highway Police was created in 1923. In 1931, the name was changed to Delaware State Police.

This 1992 Ford Taurus sports the new markings of the Delaware State Police.

A 1991 Chevy Caprice.

A 1989 Ford Crown Victoria monitoring the traffic flow.

A "Streethawk" light bar adorns this 1987 Chevy.

A sharp Dodge Diplomat shows the markings of the Delaware State Police.

An all white Chrysler Newport Sedan.

A Plymouth Gran Fury in the familiar silver and gray paint scheme.

A 4x4 Dodge pickup.

This Chevy van is used for truck enforcement duties.

A trooper strikes a pose with his 1974 Plymouth.

This 1972 Plymouth has suffered some body damage.

"Trooper Dan," a 1971 Volkswagen, is equipped with remote controlled electronics. It is used to educate preschoolers on safety issues.

A 1950 Ford with roof mounted siren and light.

This beautifully restored 1946 Ford takes part in a parade.

FLORIDA HIGHWAY PATROL

The Florida Highway Patrol was created, by law, in 1939 as the statewide traffic enforcement agency.

The current door emblem of the F.H.P.

A police dog accompanies his "partner" in this Ford.

Even though the Corvette makes an awesome cruiser, it will lose this pursuit!

A Mustang of the Florida Highway Patrol.

This Datsun 280ZX makes a unique ride!

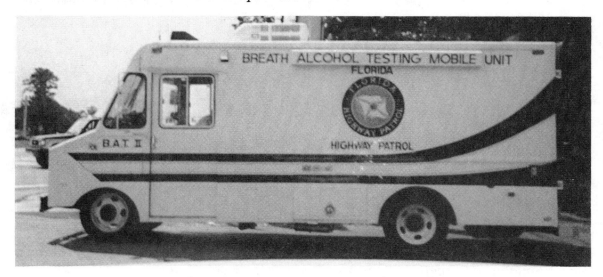

This van, commonly referred to as a BAT unit, is used for Breath Alcohol Testing.

This midsize Ford LTD is black and light yellow.

A Florida state trooper with his 1967 Plymouth. The unusual paint scheme of black and pale yellow is still used today.

This 1956 Ford features a unique paint scheme.

This photo shows the F.H.P. markings of the late 1940s. Which one of those guys do you think is having more fun?

A restored 1940 Ford Tudor sedan of the Florida Highway Patrol.

GEORGIA STATE PATROL

The Georgia Department of Public Safety was created in 1937 with the Georgia State Patrol as one of several divisions.

The current door emblem of the Georgia State Patrol.

The Georgia State Patrol uses a beautiful blue on their cruisers. Note trunk and roof markings on this Mustang.

A rear shot of the Mustang showing a close-up of the license plate.

The light bar on this Mustang has a yellow directional arrow for diverting approaching traffic.

A 1991 Ford Crown Victoria.

A 1990 Chevy Caprice photographed at Glynco, Georgia.

A state trooper with his 1953 Ford Mainline. Looks like that front end has seen some use.

IDAHO STATE POLICE

The Idaho State Police was created in 1939 with full police powers.

A Chevrolet Caprice of the Idaho State Police.

In the mid-1960s, the Idaho State Police changed its traditional black cars to light blue with white doors and roofs. This was the new door emblem at that time.

This style marking was used from the late 1940s until the mid-1960s.

This door emblem was in use in the late 1930s.

A Ford Mustang in Idaho markings.

A "slick top" Chevrolet Caprice.

A four-wheel-drive GMC Jimmy.

This mid-1980s model Plymouth has the traditional paint and markings. It includes the final marking change of moving the words "STATE POLICE" from front fenders to the stripes on the doors.

This 1978 Dodge sports the change back to black cars, now with white roofs. Note "STATE POLICE" on the front fender.

A 1961 Plymouth of the Idaho State Police.

The 1955 Chevy, often seen now with big tires and mag wheels, made a sharp looking cruiser as pictured outfitted for the Idaho State Police.

ILLINOIS STATE POLICE

The Illinois Legislature established the Illinois State Highway Patrol in 1921. Two years later, the Illinois State Highway Maintenance Police was created. The Highway Patrol was discarded in 1939 leaving only the State Highway Maintenance Police, which was transferred to the Department of Public Safety in 1941. The name was changed to Illinois State Police in 1957.

The current door emblem of the Illinois State Police.

A 1991 Chevy Caprice taking a break from patrol duties.

A "smooth top" Chevy Caprice.

A mid-1980s Dodge Diplomat. Note the gold stripes that run above and below the door emblem.

A close-up of the Dodge Diplomat's door.

This 1976 Plymouth Gran Fury is one of only twenty-four that featured special blue and red stripes in observance of our country's bicentennial.

An "on duty" photo of a 1970 Plymouth of the Illinois State Police.

A 1965 Ford Custom with a black and white paint scheme.

Illinois was one of several states to use these roof mounted "speed checks" in past years. These cars provided motorists an opportunity to check their speedometers. Shown here are rear shots of a 1959 Ford (above) and a 1965 Plymouth (below).

An all black 1938 Ford of the Illinois State Police.

These all white 1936 Ford Sedan Deliveries were used by the Illinois State Police for safety education.

INDIANA STATE POLICE

The Indiana State Police was created in 1933 as a division of the Department of Public Safety.

The current door emblem of the Indiana State Police.

This door emblem was used in the late 1980s.

This 1991 Chevy Caprice uses a Jetsonic light bar.

This 1990 Crown Victoria features eye-catching graphics.

A 1987 Ford Crown Victoria.

This 1979 Ford LTD is equipped with a roof mounted Visabar.

A 1966 Plymouth two-door sedan equipped with a single rotator on the roof and two flashers in the rear window.

A sleek 1949 Ford of the Indiana State Police.

This 1951 Pontiac cruiser has a roof mounted light and siren as well as grille lights.

IOWA STATE PATROL

In 1935, the Iowa Highway Safety Patrol was formed. In 1939, the Highway Patrol became a part of the Department of Public Safety. The name Highway Patrol was changed to State Patrol in 1973.

The current door emblem of the Iowa State Patrol.

This door emblem was used until 1973 when the name was changed to Iowa State Patrol.

A new 1994 Chevy Caprice.

This 1993 Crown Victoria currently patrols the highways around Cedar Falls, Iowa.

Rear view of a 1993 Ford Crown Victoria.

Close-up of rear markings.

The Chevys in this photo appear to be in the process of being outfitted for duty.

This tan Crown Victoria is equipped with an Aerodynic light bar and a two-way spotlight.

A variety of vehicles, including an aircraft, are shown in this 1987 photo.

A mid-1980s era tan Ford Crown Victoria.

This 1983 Plymouth Gran Fury is all white and features a remote controlled, fender mounted spotlight. Note the Iowa Department of Public Safety marking on the fender.

A 1979 Chrysler Newport.

Note the fender light on this 1965 Ford. Do you suppose this is a K-9 unit?

The only markings on this 1952 Ford appear to be the license plates.

KANSAS HIGHWAY PATROL

The Kansas Highway Patrol was established in 1937 as the state's traffic enforcement agency.

The all new door markings feature dark blue banners with yellow lettering, "KANSAS HIGHWAY PATROL," and a color state seal surrounded by stalks of wheat that are superimposed on the outline of Kansas.

A variation of the new door emblem that has an added banner that reads "TURNPIKE." This unit exclusively patrols the Kansas Turnpike.

This gold shield style door emblem was used from the 1950s to the late 1970s when it was replaced by a different shield style. The Kansas Highway Patrol used it on their cars again in the mid-1980s and early 1990s. As of 1994 it was replaced by the all new design.

This door emblem, a copy of the Kansas trooper's badge, was used in the late 1970s and early 1980s.

Among the first of the smooth top 1994 Fords, this one is silver in color with new markings.

This 1992 Ford Crown Victoria is one of the last blue/gray two-tone cars with roof light to be used. As of 1994, the KHP began using cars of various colors with no roof lights, and all new markings.

The Camaro RS has enjoyed some popularity with highway patrol agencies. This one is used by Troop B, Kansas Highway Patrol.

This 5.0-liter Ford Mustang is used by the state of Kansas.

This slick top 1991 Chevy Caprice is used for turnpike patrol.

A trooper poses with his Dodge Diplomat in Lenexa, Kansas.

A 1988 Ford Crown Victoria.

A 1988 Crown Victoria station wagon assigned to a "safety sergeant" in Hays, Kansas.

This 1987 Ford, with the now obsolete door markings, was photographed in 1989.

The 1978 Plymouth Fury was a popular cruiser of the late 1970s.

This rear shot of a Gran Fury shows rear markings, deck lights, and the "sunflower" license plate used at the time.

A 440 cubic inch V-8 rests under the hood of this 1975 Dodge Monaco.

A trooper stands at attention with his 1973 Plymouth.

This 1971 Plymouth Satellite was an unusual patrol car.

A 1970 Ford two-door hardtop used by the Kansas Highway Patrol. This particular body style was not commonly used for patrol cars.

A 1966 Plymouth Belvedere two-door sedan.

A 1962 Dodge Dart of the K.H.P.

Two Kansas cruisers, a 1960 Dodge with a 1959 Plymouth in the background.

These two 1959 Plymouths appear to be involved in a training exercise.

An original patrol car of the Kansas Highway Patrol, a 1937 Plymouth.

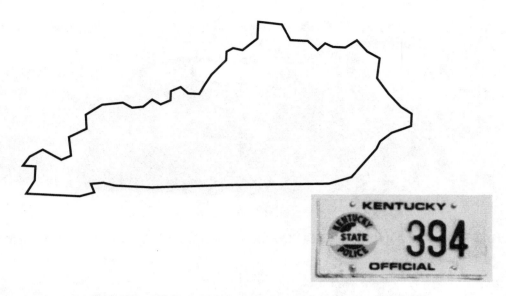

KENTUCKY STATE POLICE

The Kentucky State Highway Patrol originated in 1936. It was changed to Kentucky State Police in 1948.

The current door emblem of the Kentucky State Police.

This 1994 Ford Crown Victoria is medium blue, with dark blue stripe and lettering, "State Trooper."

This Ford Crown Victoria wears a single blue rotator.

This white Crown Victoria was photographed while refueling.

A 1980 Dodge St. Regis flanked by a 1979 Ford LTD.

A 1973 Ford in front of the Kentucky State Police headquarters building.

This 1964 Plymouth two-door sedan was used by the Kentucky State Police.

1960 Plymouths photographed at curbside with an unknown group.

Distinctive lettering highlights the rear of this 1949 Chevy Sedan Delivery.

A rocky formation serves as a backdrop for this trooper and his 1950 Ford.

A beautifully restored 1949 Ford two-door sedan of the Kentucky State Police. Door emblem is gold and white with a corresponding gold stripe. Note fender mounted red lights.

Rear view of the restored 1949 Ford.

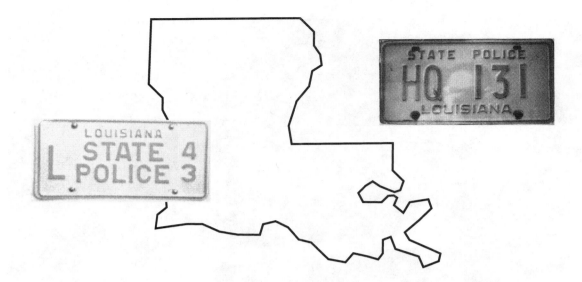

LOUISIANA STATE POLICE

The Louisiana State Highway Patrol was created in 1932. The Department of State Police, established in 1936, included the Highway Patrol and the Criminal Identification Bureau.

This is a close-up of the previous style door emblem used on dark blue L.S.P. vehicles of the late 1980s.

This new 1994 Chevy Caprice is currently patrolling the highways of Louisiana.

This Ford station wagon serves as a crime scene investigation unit.

The ever present Ford Mustang!

The all blue light bar seems to blend in with the dark blue paint on this Crown Victoria. The 1990s see the return of the all white cruisers of the Louisiana State Police.

A Dodge Ramcharger for "hard to reach" places.

This armored vehicle looks as if it could withstand the rigors of war instead of police work. Note the gun ports under the small windows.

An armored vehicle used for tactical situations.

A late 1980s Chevy Caprice.

This big Ford was ready to roll in 1976.

This 1954 Ford of the Louisiana State Police used the roof mounted siren and light that was popular in the 1950s and 1960s.

MAINE STATE POLICE

The Maine State Police was established by law in 1925.

The current door emblem of the Maine State Police.

The Maine State Police use a sharp blue on their cars. Pictured is a 1991 Chevy Caprice.

This Chevy uses a blue strobe type light bar.

An older style strobe-type light bar sits atop this Chevy.

Folks might have missed this unmarked 1957 Studebaker of the Maine State Police. A keen eye can see the whip antenna and license plates.

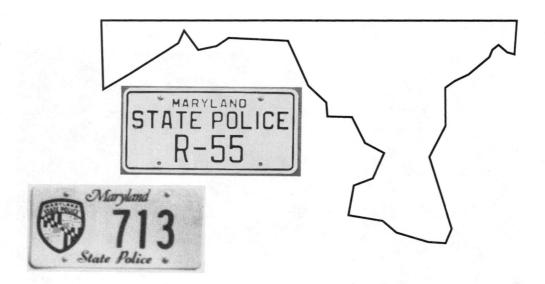

MARYLAND STATE POLICE

The Maryland State Police was created in 1920 to enforce laws statewide.

The current door emblem of the Maryland State Police.

This triangular door emblem was used in the 1940s. It matched the uniform shoulder patch worn at the time.

A 1992 Ford Taurus currently in service.

A 1991 Chevy Caprice with the current tan paint.

A 1989 Chevy Caprice, unit "T-11."

This Chevy Blazer is used for a K-9 unit.

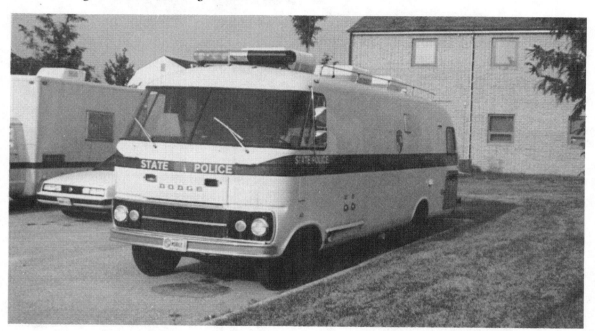

A Dodge motorhome used for a mobile command post.

Note the unusual light bar on this GMC bus.

The license plate on this CJ-5 Jeep indicates it belongs to a tactical unit.

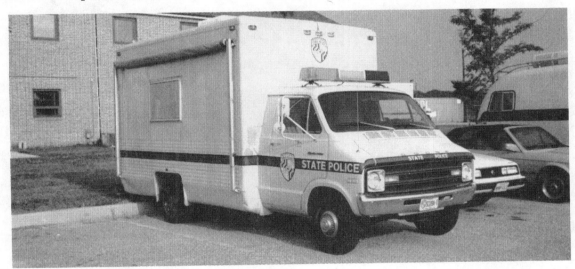

This Dodge Cube Van is used by the Scuba unit.

This Ford Club Wagon van is towing a trailer used for an on-site command center.

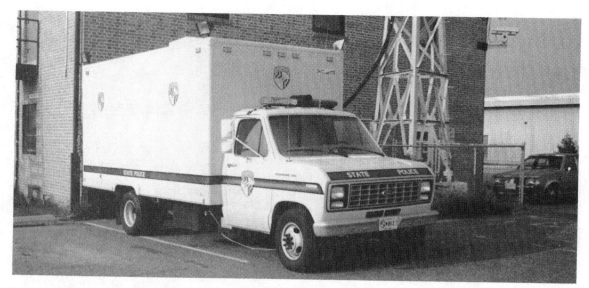

The license plate on this Ford truck reads "MOBILE." Note the lights on the top of the box for on-scene illumination.

This Jeep pickup first saw service with the military.

The popular Ford Crown Victoria of the 1980s.

This Chevy box van was photographed in the late 1970s. Maryland State Police vehicles were light yellow at that time.

This Plymouth Fury is a 1977 model.

A 1976 Plymouth Gran Fury station wagon.

A 1970 Torino.

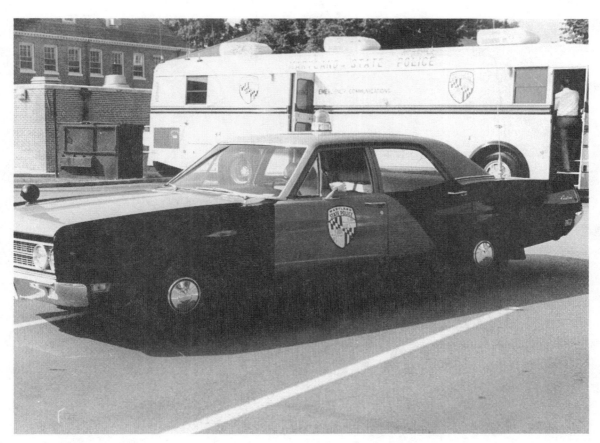

A restored 1969 Ford of the Maryland State Police.

A big 1967 Chevy tow-truck.

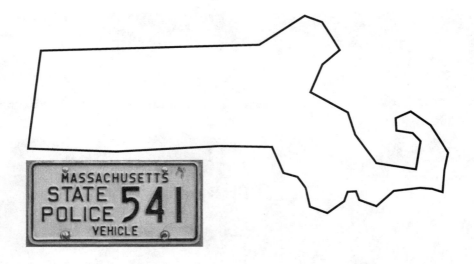

MASSACHUSETTS STATE POLICE

The Massachusetts State Police was officially formed in 1921.

The current door emblem of the Massachusetts State Police.

This Ford Crown Victoria is the new style 1992.

Note the large bumper on this Chevy Suburban.

Massachusetts State Police vehicles have a unique dark blue and gray paint scheme. The cruiser pictured is a 1989 Ford Crown Victoria.

A Chevy van used by the Massachusetts State Police Drill Team.

This mid-1970s Ford is outfitted with an Aerodynic light bar.

A 1967 Ford two-door sedan.

A pair of 1957 Ford two-doors at a state police garage.

A trooper poses with his 1961 Ford two-door sedan.

MICHIGAN STATE POLICE

The Michigan State Police was organized in 1919.

The current door emblem of the Michigan State Police.

137

A 1992 Chevy Caprice "slick top."

This 1992 Camaro RS features front end red lights instead of a light bar.

Part of the door molding on this 1988 Ford Mustang was removed to accommodate the door shield.

A 1987 Chevy Caprice with the unique hood mounted "STOP" sign used by the Michigan State Police.

A 1978 Plymouth Fury of the Michigan State Police.

A Ford truck used by the Emergency Services Team.

This smooth top Dodge Diplomat utilizes front mounted red lights.

The Chevy Impala was a standard police cruiser before the Caprice. This one is a 1978 model.

A choice looking 1957 Ford two-door sedan.

MINNESOTA STATE PATROL

1929 marked the year that the Minnesota State Highway Patrol was organized. The name was changed from Highway Patrol to State Patrol in 1979.

This door emblem, used for many years, was replaced in 1992 by the new graphics.

New graphics appeared in 1992, as shown on this Ford Crown Victoria.

A Chevy Caprice, in the traditional maroon color of the Minnesota State Patrol, features red lights mounted on the push bars.

A Jetsonic light bar as well as front reds are used on this Chevrolet Caprice.

This 1985 Plymouth Gran Fury features the old style Visabar with twin rotators.

This van was used as a mobile communications unit until 1988.

A trooper and his big Plymouth Gran Fury.

This restored Model A Ford coupe displays the door marking of that era.

MISSISSIPPI HIGHWAY SAFETY PATROL

The Mississippi Highway Safety Patrol was one of two divisions formed as part of the Department of Public Safety in 1938.

The current door emblem of the Mississippi Highway Safety Patrol.

This trooper stands with his 1992 Ford Crown Victoria.

A 1990s Ford Mustang with the currently used markings of the Mississippi Highway Safety Patrol.

This 1990 Ford Crown Victoria is white with a blue stripe.

A distinctive blue 1977 Plymouth Gran Fury with blue lights that are traditionally used in southern states.

A museum display showing a 1937 Ford two-door sedan with Mississippi Highway Safety Patrol markings. Note the evolution of the uniforms as displayed on mannequins posed with the car.

MISSOURI STATE HIGHWAY PATROL

The Missouri State Highway Patrol was created by law in 1931.

The current door emblem of the Missouri State Highway Patrol.

This close-up shows the currently used markings for the door and fender, and the circular Sixtieth Anniversary decal of the Missouri State Highway Patrol.

This emblem, a variation of the original, was used from the late 1930s until 1942. From 1942 to 1947, the door emblem consisted of bold words that read simply "STATE PATROL."

The original door emblem used by the Missouri State Highway Patrol.

A 1992 Ford Crown Victoria.

This smooth top 1992 Ford Crown Victoria is used as a K-9 unit.

License plates used through the years. These are on display at the State Highway Patrol Museum in Jefferson City, Missouri.

This 1991 Chevy Caprice is dark blue in color.

A 1991 Chevy Caprice wagon with D.A.R.E. (Drug Abuse Resistance Education) markings.

Missouri is a state that uses various colored cruisers as shown with this silver 1991 Chevy Caprice and dark gray Crown Victoria.

An attractive blue 5.0-liter Ford Mustang.

This D.A.R.E. marked unit is a Ford.

This 1985 Crown Victoria is tan in color.

This armored tactical unit looks like its military counterpart.

A 1976 Plymouth Gran Fury with old style light bar.

MONTANA HIGHWAY PATROL

The Montana Highway Patrol was formed in 1935 to enforce laws statewide.

The current door emblem of the Montana Highway Patrol.

This 1993 Ford Crown Victoria is currently in service.

A blue 1991 Chevy Caprice parked on a lonely Montana highway.

This 1987 Chevy Impala is all white.

Close-up of the door emblem on the 1987 Chevy.

This Plymouth Gran Fury was photographed in 1986 with a 1935 Ford coupe restored to represent an original patrol car of the Montana Highway Patrol.

A trooper standing in front of a 1955 Ford. Note the small star door emblem.

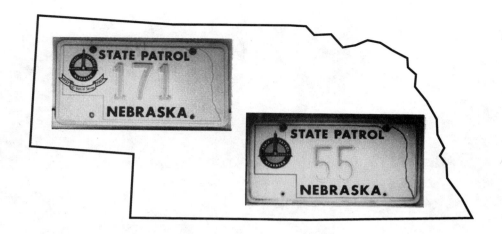

NEBRASKA STATE PATROL

The Nebraska Safety Patrol was created by legislature in 1937. The name Safety Patrol was changed to State Patrol in 1967.

The current door emblem of the Nebraska State Patrol.

The original door emblem that was used from 1937 to the early 1940s. A down-sized version of the same basic emblem was used in the late 1940s.

A new Ford Bronco in service as a K-9 unit.

A Jetsonic light bar is used on this 1992 Ford.

The Camaro RS pictured is one of a small number currently being used by the Nebraska State Patrol.

Rear view of the Camaro RS featuring "STATE PATROL" markings.

The Ford Mustang of the 1990s has changed little since its law enforcement debut in 1982 and it is still a popular patrol car.

A late 1980s Crown Victoria.

The emblem on the fender designates this Chevy was used by a D.A.R.E. officer.

A Ford Aerostar van used by the Safety Education Unit of the N.S.P.

This GMC Safari van is also a Safety Education unit.

"Ford got the state bid in 1986."

Patrol cars wore a special fender decal as part of the Fiftieth Anniversary celebration, shown on this Dodge Diplomat.

The Nebraska State Patrol decided to test the Ford Mustang in 1985. Shown here is one of the original thirty purchased for just over $9,000 each.

A slick 1977 Dodge Monaco two-door photographed on Interstate 80.

This 1977 Plymouth Gran Fury was photographed on the state fairgrounds in Lincoln, Nebraska.

In the early 1970s, the N.S.P. broke away from its use of all white cruisers and opted for variously colored ones. Pictured is a brown 1972 Ford two-door model.

1963 marked the first year of the all white patrol cars for the Nebraska Safety Patrol. This patrolman poses with his 1963 Ford.

A 1961 Dodge of the Nebraska Safety Patrol.

A 1950 Buick Jetback of the Nebraska Safety Patrol.

A mechanic preparing a 1952 Ford for patrol. Note the grille mounted red light and "NEBRASKA STATE CAR" license plate.

This 1950 Ford used a red light mounted in the centerpiece of the grille as well as a fender mounted "STOP" light.

NEVADA HIGHWAY PATROL

Although a Nevada State Police was formed in 1908, little is known of their duties. The Nevada Highway Patrol was established in 1949.

The current door emblem of the Nevada Highway Patrol.

A 1991 Camaro RS with a more aerodynamic version of the short light bar.

A 1989 Ford Mustang in "off duty" mode.

This Plymouth Gran Fury was photographed in 1983.

The dark gray and blue used by the Nevada Highway Patrol is striking! The short light bar shown on this Chevy is widely used in Nevada.

The forerunner of the 1980s Diplomat and Gran Fury models was the Chrysler LeBaron. This one was in service in Nevada around 1981.

This Dodge pickup is used for commercial vehicle equipment enforcement duties.

This sharp 1977 Pontiac LeMans was used in Nevada.

A 1946-48 Chrysler "black and white" used by the Nevada Highway Patrol.

NEW HAMPSHIRE STATE POLICE

The New Hampshire State Police was organized in 1937 as a statewide law enforcement agency.

The current door emblem of the New Hampshire State Police.

New Hampshire State Police vehicles are currently an impressive dark green and copper. Pictured is a 1991 Ford.

This Chevy, photographed in the rain, used blue strobe roof lights.

This Ford Crown Victoria was photographed at the Manchester Police Department.

A 1975 Pontiac Catalina of the New Hampshire State Police.

This state police sergeant was assigned to a 1953 Desoto.

A dashing trooper with his 1942 Dodge coupe. Note the unusual radio antenna.

State Police motorcycle officers posed for a photo in the late 1930s.

NEW JERSEY STATE POLICE

The New Jersey State Police was created by law in 1921.

The current door emblem of the New Jersey State Police.

Note the push bars on the front of this 1991 Chevy Caprice.

This GMC truck is used as a unit of the bomb squad.

This Chevy is outfitted with a Streethawk light bar.

An Aerodynic light bar adorns the roof of this 1987 Ford Crown Victoria.

A Dodge van of the New Jersey State Police.

An immaculately uniformed state police officer posed with his 1978 Ford LTD II.

A 1973 Mercury in the black and white paint scheme used at that time. Note the white wheels.

Note the peculiar roof light on this 1951 Ford. The door emblem reads "NEW JER-SEY TURNPIKE AUTHORITY."

This "black and white" of the 1940s has plain lettering and no door emblem.

NEW MEXICO STATE POLICE

The New Mexico Motor Patrol was formed in 1933. In 1935, the Motor Patrol reorganized into the State Police.

The current door emblem of the New Mexico State Police.

A black and white 1988 Chevy Caprice of the New Mexico State Police.

This Ford Crown Victoria utilizes red lights on the push bar instead of a light bar.

State policeman with his 1954 Ford. This car features front and rear facing roof lights.

A 1980 Dodge St. Regis with an old style Visabar with dual rotators.

The rear view of this 1954 Ford shows the use of the door shield as a marking on the trunk lid.

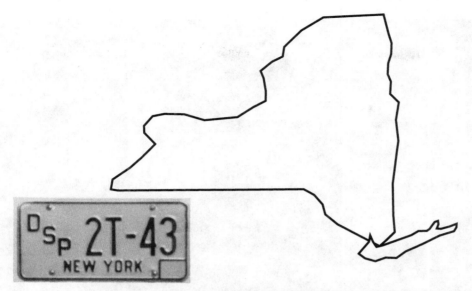

NEW YORK STATE POLICE

The New York State Police was created in 1917. Horses were the agency's primary "cruiser" at this time.

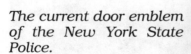
The current door emblem of the New York State Police.

New York's version of the Camaro RS.

Current N.Y.S.P. vehicles are dark blue, as is this 1991 Chevy Caprice.

A 1990 Ford Crown Victoria.

This 1989 Ford Mustang was photographed at Buffalo, New York.

A 1987 Chevrolet of the New York State Police

The style of light bar shown on this 1987 Crown Victoria is no longer used by the N.Y.S.P.

This Chevy Blazer takes care of four-wheel-drive needs.

Another four-wheel-drive, this one a Dodge Ramcharger.

A Dodge van in the familiar role as a commercial vehicle enforcement unit.

A yellow over blue Plymouth Gran Fury photographed in the mid-1980s.

Close-up of markings of mid-1980s Plymouth.

The striking yellow and blue paint scheme on this 1974 Dodge Monaco was quite noticeable!

1973 was the first year N.Y.S.P. used yellow and blue cars as modeled on this Mercury Monterey.

This 1973 Plymouth sports the older blue over white paint scheme.

An aviation accident brought this 1955 Ford to the scene. The car was white with a dark blue roof and hood.

This trooper had a young assistant as he changed the headlight on his 1957 Ford cruiser.

A restored 1946 Ford of the New York State Police.

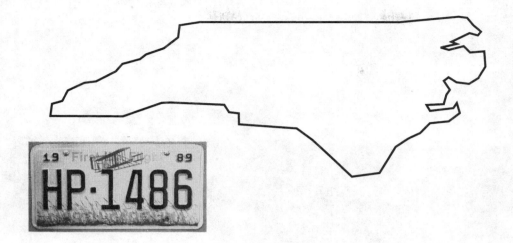

NORTH CAROLINA HIGHWAY PATROL

1929 was the year the North Carolina Highway Patrol was organized.

The current door emblem of the North Carolina Highway Patrol.

A currently used 1991 Chevy Caprice.

Ford Crown Victoria for 1988.

This 4x4 Ford Bronco features a front mounted winch.

This Chevrolet pickup is the standard black and silver.

No blue lights are visible on this Ford Mustang.

A mid-1980s Ford Crown Victoria.

A trooper poses with his 1978 Chevy Impala.

The following five photos show cars that are owned by the North Carolina Highway Patrol and reside in the North Carolina Transportation Museum. They were restored by the maintenance section at the N.C.H.P. fleet garage in Raleigh.

This 1984 Mustang GT convertible was donated by an admirer of the highway patrol.

This 1977 Plymouth Fury has a single blue rotator on top.

This 1969 Ford has a roof mounted siren with a blue light.

1941 Ford coupe in black and silver.

A 1929 Model A Ford coupe that represents the highway patrol's original cars.

NORTH DAKOTA
HIGHWAY PATROL

The North Dakota Highway Patrol was formed in 1935 as its statewide traffic enforcement agency.

The current door emblem of the North Dakota State Patrol honors Red Tomahawk, a Sioux Indian policeman involved in the capture of Chief Sitting Bull.

A currently used 1992 Ford Crown Victoria.

A 1990 Chevy Blazer in the current style markings.

A 1989 Ford Crown Victoria from North Dakota. Note "Trooper of the Year" designation above the fender marking. Color is all white with brown and gold stripes.

This 1988 Plymouth Gran Fury has the old style brown paint.

This 1987 Dodge Ramcharger is used for mobile weight enforcement.

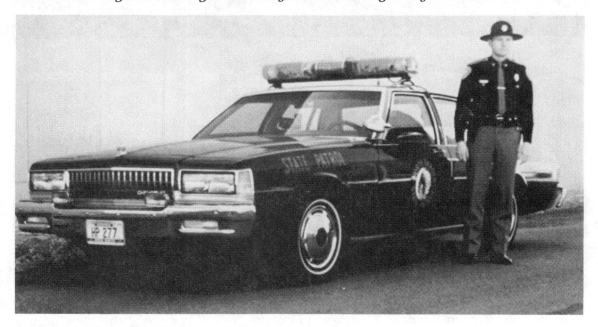

An Aerodynic light bar sits atop this patrol unit.

The North Dakota state capital in Fargo is pictured in the background behind this trooper and his 1972 Oldsmobile. The car is blue in color.

Car #5 of the North Dakota Highway Patrol, a 1937 Studebaker coupe.

The original five members of the North Dakota Highway Patrol in 1935. The cars are 1935 Buick Series 40 coupes.

OHIO STATE HIGHWAY PATROL

Organization of the Ohio State Highway Patrol occurred in 1933.

The current door emblem of the Ohio State Highway Patrol.

Silver gray is the standard color used by the Ohio State Highway Patrol. Note the special license plate on this 1991 Ford Crown Victoria.

Chevrolets being prepared for service.

This Plymouth is decked out in red and blue stripes in celebration of our country's bicentennial.

This 1974 Chevy Impala has a simple rotator on the roof.

This 1965 Ford marked the last year of black patrol cars for the Ohio Highway Patrol. The department's 1966 Fords were all white.

A black 1962 Chevy two-door sedan.

A 1958 Chevrolet Delray two-door. This car belonged to the Ohio Highway Patrol. Chevrolets of this vintage were plagued by poor brakes.

The Hudson Hornet made a unique patrol car.

A patrolman proudly stands beside his 1938 Ford convertible. It looks like a fun patrol car!

OKLAHOMA HIGHWAY PATROL

The Oklahoma Department of Public Safety was formed in 1937 with the Highway Patrol as one of its divisions.

The current door emblem of the Oklahoma Highway Patrol.

This mid-1950s photo shows a slight variation of the current markings on Oklahoma Highway Patrol cars.

This smooth-top Chevy Caprice features a unique style of black and white paint scheme. A trademark of sorts, on Oklahoma Highway Patrol vehicles is the added white paint over rear wheel wells.

The 1991 Chevy Caprice.

This Chevy is outfitted with a Jetstream light bar.

A Plymouth Gran Fury with the single rotator, used up to the late 1980s.

Ford's Mustang in service in Oklahoma in the mid-1980s.

An all white Plymouth Gran Fury.

A Plymouth Gran Fury for 1980.

OREGON STATE POLICE

The Oregon State Police, created in 1931, performs police functions on a statewide level.

1994 marked the first major change in vehicle markings in over forty years. This Chevy Caprice displays the all new paint and markings of the Oregon State Police. The change is a great improvement!

The Camaro RS in Oregon State Police markings.

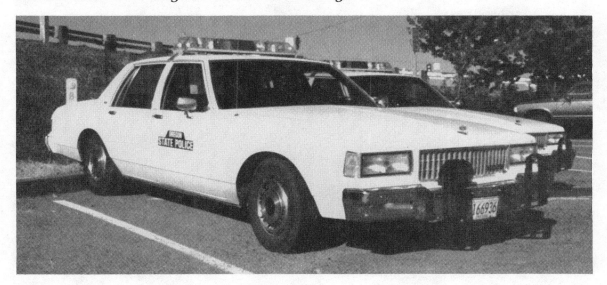

This pair of Chevys await their next shift.

The Fish and Wildlife Service is a part of the state police. The game wardens use pickups such as the Ford 4x4.

A 1985 Ford LTD.

Note the small red and blue lights on the roof of this Ford Mustang.

A trooper poses with his 1979 Chrysler Newport.

A 1952 Ford Mainline two-door sedan.

This trooper took time from his duties to pose for a photo with his 1941 Ford coupe. Note the state seal door emblem that was used in the early years.

PENNSYLVANIA STATE POLICE

State law enforcement started in Pennsylvania in 1905 with two agencies, a State Police and a State Highway Patrol. In 1937, these agencies combined to form the Pennsylvania Motor Police. The organization changed somewhat in 1943 and was renamed the Pennsylvania State Police.

The current door emblem of the Pennsylvania State Police.

This 1992 Chevy Caprice is currently in use and is outfitted with a new Vision lightbar.

A 1991 Crown Victoria is white with blue trim and markings.

A 1989 Chevy Caprice.

This Jeep Cherokee is equipped with a grille guard and winch.

This Ford Crown Victoria is a 1986 model.

A close-up of the door markings in the 1986 Ford.

A group of Plymouth Gran Furys and Dodge St. Regis of the Pennsylvania State Police.

This photo shows rear end markings on the blue and white Plymouth.

This 1982 Chevy Malibu had a slightly different door emblem and no side stripe as seen on late 1980s units.

Close-up of the Malibu's door emblem.

This 1973 Plymouth has a blue and yellow paint scheme.

The Pennsylvania State Police cars have had several color variations, such as this 1963 Ford, which is green and white.

Note the markings on the door and above the windshield on this 1950 Ford.

These all white 1937 Fords have simple markings that read "STATE POLICE."

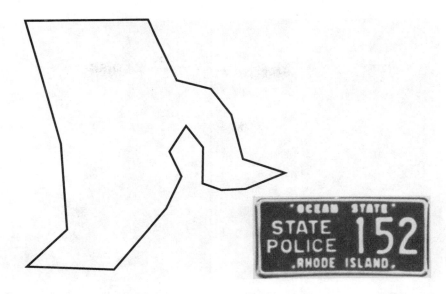

RHODE ISLAND STATE POLICE

The Rhode Island State Police was created by law in 1925.

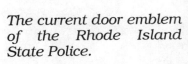

The current door emblem of the Rhode Island State Police.

This 1992 Ford is the standard gray of the Rhode Island State Police.

There is no question as to the identity of this Ford with three "STATE POLICE" markings on each side of it.

This mid-1980s Ford Crown Victoria uses a Jetsonic light bar.

224

SOUTH CAROLINA HIGHWAY PATROL

1930 marked the year that the South Carolina Highway Patrol began service.

The current door emblem of the South Carolina Highway Patrol.

A 1990 Ford Crown Victoria of the South Carolina Highway Patrol.

This Ford Mustang is equipped with a blue strobe light bar.

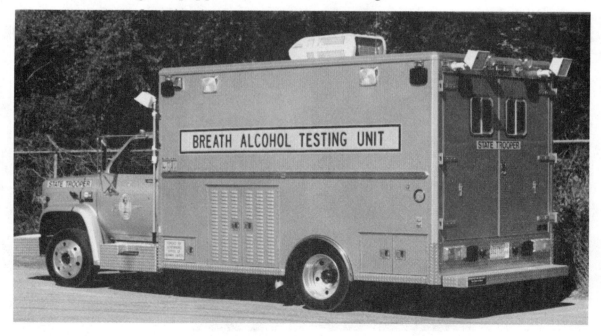

The Governor's Office of Highway Safety funded this heavy-duty Breath Alcohol Testing unit.

This mid-1980s Ford is silver with blue stripes and gold emblems.

A trooper pictured with his late-1970s Ford.

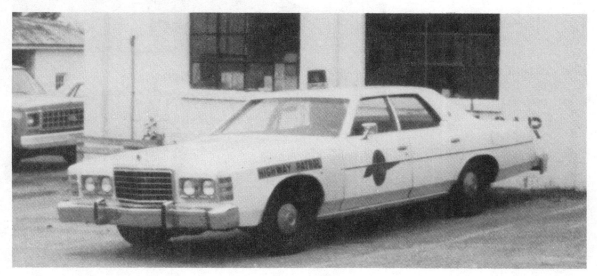

This 1976 Ford is white with standard blue light.

SOUTH DAKOTA
HIGHWAY PATROL

Although earlier attempts at forming a state traffic enforcement agency occurred, the South Dakota Highway Patrol was formally organized in 1938.

The current door emblem of the South Dakota Highway Patrol.

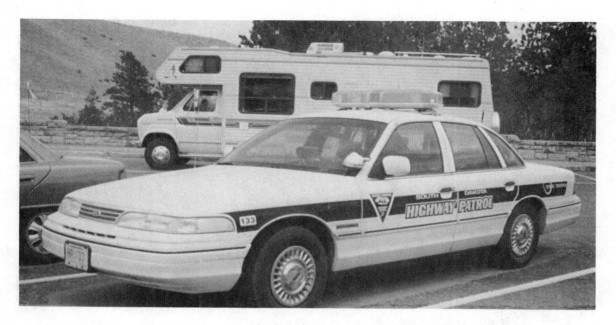

A 1994 Ford Crown Victoria featuring the new graphics of the South Dakota Highway Patrol.

Rear view of the South Dakota Crown Victoria.

This door emblem was used by the South Dakota Highway Patrol prior to August of 1993.

The previous style markings are shown on this light blue and white 1992 Ford Crown Victoria.

A mid-1980s Crown Victoria.

This 1983 Ford was photographed at Buffalo, South Dakota.

A 1979 Plymouth Gran Fury.

TENNESSEE HIGHWAY PATROL

The Tennessee Highway Patrol was established in 1929 to perform statewide traffic enforcement duties.

This 1991 Chevy Caprice displays all new markings.

This trooper posed proudly with his black and white Plymouth Gran Fury. The markings are quite impressive.

A Chevy van used by the Tennessee Highway Patrol.

This style of door emblem was used by the Tennessee Highway Patrol for many years up to the 1990s.

The Tennessee "Litter Bug" is used for litter prevention programs.

A 1980 Plymouth Gran Fury.

This 1979 Chrysler Newport is equipped with a blue strobe light bar. The "1979" denotes the Tennessee Highway Patrol's Fiftieth Anniversary.

This 1978 Plymouth is outfitted with a Visabar with twin blue rotators.

A 1954 Ford Mainline on patrol duty. Note the former style markings.

TEXAS HIGHWAY PATROL

The Texas Highway Patrol was formally organized in 1931. The Texas Department of Public Safety, formed in 1935, was originally comprised of the Highway Patrol and the Texas Rangers.

The current door emblem of the Texas Highway Patrol.

The door emblem of the 1980s was basically the same as the current style except the words "HIGHWAY PATROL" were moved to the top of the emblem.

This photo illustrates the state-shaped door emblem of the 1950s.

The door emblem of the 1930s and 1940s resembled the badge worn on patrolmen uniforms.

A currently used Chevy Caprice of the Texas Highway Patrol.

"Cruising" in style, the Camaro RS on patrol.

A 5.0-liter Ford Mustang on duty.

This Ford is used by the Drivers License Division of the Texas Department of Public Safety.

These 1979 Chrysler Newports have red and blue rotators.

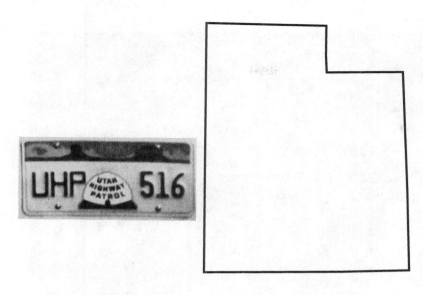

UTAH HIGHWAY PATROL

The Utah Highway Patrol was formally organized and named in 1928.

The current door emblem of the Utah Highway Patrol.

Current patrol cars of the Utah Highway Patrol: Camaro RS, Ford Taurus, and Ford Mustang.

This Ford Mustang is equipped with a blue and red strobe light bar.

The twin spotlights on this Ford Mustang are quite noticeable.

A smooth top Dodge Diplomat of the Utah Highway Patrol.

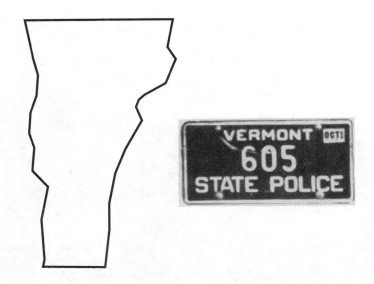

VERMONT STATE POLICE

The Department of Public Safety was created in 1947 with the Vermont State Police as one division.

The current door emblem of the Vermont State Police.

Prior to the 1990s, the Vermont State Police door emblem was used with no other markings.

Vermont State Police cars are a deep green with a gold stripe. Shown here is a 1991 Chevy Caprice.

A pair of Chevrolets ready for patrol.

A state trooper posed with his Plymouth Gran Fury on a beautiful autumn day.

This mid-1980s Plymouth Gran Fury has the prior style paint scheme, gold over green.

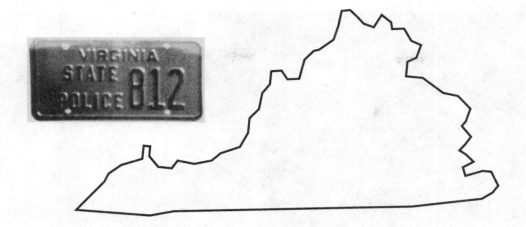

VIRGINIA STATE POLICE

Although Division of Motor Vehicles Inspectors had full police powers as early as 1932, the actual Virginia State Police was formed in 1942.

The current door emblem of the Virginia State Police.

This blue and gray cruiser is a 1991 Chevy Caprice.

A sharp 1987 Chevy Caprice with single blue rotator.

This heavy-duty GMC truck is used for bomb disposal duties.

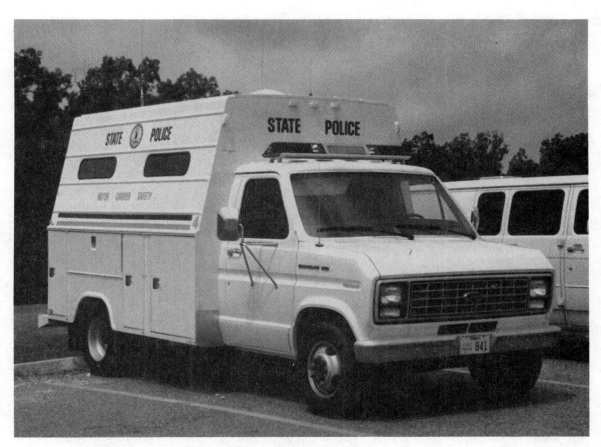

This Ford truck is marked "MOTOR CARRIER SAFETY."

A Dodge modular van used for crime scene evidence collection duties.

A red rotator was used on this 1977 Plymouth Fury. The Virginia State Police currently use blue lights.

Plymouth Fury for 1974.

A 1973 Plymouth with a small red rotator.

WASHINGTON STATE PATROL

State traffic enforcement duties began in 1921 with the Washington State Highway Patrol. The agency was reorganized and renamed the Washington State Patrol in 1933.

The current door emblem of the Washington State Patrol.

This 1991 Chevy Caprice is equipped with a push bar and blue lights on the roof.

This Chevy Caprice was photographed at a detachment headquarters.

In addition to a blue and red light bar, this Ford Mustang is outfitted with a two-way spotlight.

This Ford LTD was a mid-size cruiser.

This mid-1980s Ford Mustang has a red and blue Jetsonic light bar.

This preserved Plymouth Fury has the distinction of being the last cruiser of the Washington State Patrol to have a 440 cubic inch engine.

A 1968 Chevrolet of the Washington State Patrol.

1962 Dodges such as this were powered by either a 318 or 361 cubic inch engine putting out up to 305 horsepower.

This 1960 Ford carried quite an array of equipment.

A run of bad luck for this 1936 Ford panel truck!

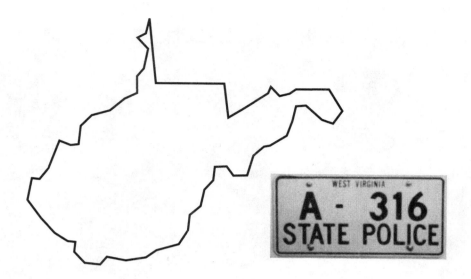

WEST VIRGINIA STATE POLICE

The West Virginia State Police, established in 1919, originally had only criminal law enforcement duties. Traffic enforcement duties were not assigned to the State Police until 1929.

The current door emblem of the West Virginia State Police.

A blue strobe light bar sits on top of this Ford.

How about spending your shift patrolling in this Dodge Daytona?

This Dodge Diplomat has red and blue lenses on the high-beam headlights.

This smooth top Dodge Diplomat is silver in color.

This Dodge Diplomat uses an Aerodynic light bar.

Gold over dark blue are the colors of this 1975 Plymouth.

WISCONSIN STATE PATROL

The Wisconsin State Traffic Patrol originated in 1939. The name was changed to State Patrol in the late 1950s.

The current door emblem of the Wisconsin State Patrol.

A smooth top 1992 Ford Crown Victoria.

Jetsonic light bar and push bars appear on this 1991 Chevy Caprice.

A beautiful blue Camaro RS wearing the emblems of the Wisconsin State Patrol.

This Mustang is marked with a Fiftieth Anniversary emblem just ahead of the rear wheel well.

A trooper photographed with his 1988 Ford Mustang.

Rear view of 1988 Ford Mustang shows miniature red and blue rotators mounted in the rear window. The license plate has been replaced with a new style.

A slick top Plymouth Gran Fury equipped with two-way spotlight.

An unusual cruiser, this 1957 Rambler is outfitted with a single rotating roof light and fender mounted siren.

Note the now obsolete style door emblem on the panel truck, which reads "WISCON-SIN STATE TRAFFIC PATROL." The license plate on the 1951 Ford reads the same.

The door shield on this restored 1939 Ford reads "STATE TRAFFIC PATROL-MOTOR VEHICLE DEPARTMENT-WIS."

WYOMING HIGHWAY PATROL

Although a handful of state traffic officers were appointed in 1933, the Wyoming Highway Patrol officially started in 1935. The name was changed to the Wyoming Cowboy Courtesy Patrol for a short time during the 1940s. The title Wyoming Highway Patrol was restored and remains so today.

The current door emblem of the Wyoming Highway Patrol.

This 1994 Chevy Camaro is one of eleven used by the Wyoming Highway Patrol.

Awesome would be one way to describe this view of the Camaro in your rear view mirror!

The trooper's badge number as well as the special "HP" highway patrol license plate appear on both ends of the Wyoming Camaro.

This 1993 Ford Crown Victoria is currently in service with the Wyoming Highway Patrol.

An eye-catching Camaro RS in the standard white over black colors of the Wyoming Highway Patrol.

A blue and red Jetsonic light bar sits atop this Crown Victoria. The unit number is mounted on the grille.

A 1988 Chevy Caprice.

A 1987 Ford Crown Victoria.

A black and white 1976 Ford complete with patrolman.

This 1973 Chevy Impala used a Visabar with twin red rotators.

This 1971 Buick LeSabre is powered by a 400 cubic inch engine. It is marked with the former style door emblem that features a buffalo surrounded by the words "WYOMING HIGHWAY PATROL".

Factory Brochures Offer 'Best On Any Beat'

"America's Badge of Authority", "Here's the Ticket for Police Duty", "Best on Any Beat", "America's No. 1 Police Car". No matter how clever the slogan, bottom line was sales. These examples were found on the cover of factory police car brochures that were and still are used to sell prospective customers. The automakers distributed these brochures to dealers around the country. They were heavily illustrated and often contained fifteen or more pages. Many options were offered, particularly in engine size. Various body styles were shown that were adorned with the emblems of certain major law enforcement agencies who apparently already had these cars in service.

Today these colorful brochures have diminished to a multi-page list of specifications, with a token photo or two. Gone are the various choices of body styles, the markings of actual departments and those great catch-phrases! Their purpose is the same however, to garner sales.

These brochures are interesting and affordable collectibles today. Reasonably priced brochures can often be found at collectors shows and automotive swap meets. They can be purchased from dealers in advertising materials as well. Cost varies from a few dollars for modern brochures to between $5 and $20 for older pre-1980 examples. Some older and more rare copies are usually more expensive.

(What follows is a sampling of "Police Package" features and options from "Big Three" brochures for fourteen models so equipped and offered for sale.)

1963 CHEVROLET POLICE CARS

Eight Engines

425-HP TURBO-FIRE 409 V-8 power-packed 409-cu. in. displacement, 11.0:1 compression ratio, twin four-barrel carburetors, dual exhaust, dry-element air cleaner, cast aluminum intake manifold, special camshaft with mechanical valve lifters, tough-surface crankshaft bearings and extra-strong pistons. Cylinder heads feature large valves and smooth ports. Automatic choke, full-flow oil filter, temperature-controlled fan.

400-HP TURBO-FIRE 409 V-8 delivers 425 lb.-ft. maximum torque. 409 cu.-in. displacement, 11.0:1 compression ratio, large four-barrel aluminum carburetor. Oil-wetted element air cleaner.

NEW 340-HP TURBO-FIRE 409 V-8 Engine that's ideal for modern police use. 409 cu.-in. displacement, 10.1:1 compression ratio, single four-barrel carburetor, hydraulic valve lifters, regular camshaft. Dry-element air cleaner.

300-HP TURBO-FIRE 327 V-8 327 cu.-in. displacement, 10.5:1 compression ratio, large four-barrel aluminum carburetor, plus special free-breathing characteristics. Additional Turbo-Fire 327 features include temperature-controlled fan, full-pressure lubrication with full-flow filter, hydraulic valve lifters, automatic choke, dry-type air cleaner and dual exhaust.

250-HP TURBO-FIRE 327 V-8 327 cu.-in. displacement, 10.5:1 compression ratio, regular four-barrel carburetor. Includes most other Turbo-Fire 327 features listed above.

SPECIAL 230-HP TURBO-FIRE 327 V-8 special cylinder heads afford substantial savings on fuel costs with little sacrifice in performance. 327 cu.-in. displacement, 8.6:1 compression ratio, four-barrel carburetor, plus other Turbo-Fire 327 basic features.

IMPROVED 195-HP TURBO-FIRE 283 V-8 - Chevrolet's standard V-8 delivers 25 more horse-power than last year's for sparkling performance on regular gas. Higher lift camshaft allows better engine breathing. Slightly smaller combustion chambers increase compression ratio for more power. Special damper springs control valve spring surge. 283 cu.-in. displacement, 9.25:1 compression ratio, two-barrel carburetor, full-pressure lubrication, dry-element air cleaner, single exhaust.

ALL-NEW 140-HP TURBO-THRIFT 230 SIX - Here's one of the most efficient 6-cylinder engines. Seven main bearings for exceptional sturdiness and smoothness. Modern short-stroke design with modified wedge combustion chambers. Full-pressure lubrication and full-flow oil filter. New automatic choke gives more precise response to engine requirements. 230 cu.-in. displacement, 8.5:1 compression ratio, single-barrel carburetor, oil-wetted air cleaner.

Four Transmissions
3-SPEED SYNCHRO-MESH - Standard transmission for all Chevrolet engines. Allhelical gear design with high torque capacity.

NEW POWERGLIDE - Accelerator-triggered downshift gives surge of power whenever needed. Aluminum housing cuts weight for improved performance.

4-SPEED SYNCHRO-MESH - All forward gears are synchronized to permit rapid downshifts for bursts of acceleration. Floor-mounted shift lever.

OVERDRIVE - Overdrive unit is teamed with Chevrolet's rugged 3-Speed Synchro-Mesh transmission.

1963 CHEVROLET POLICE CAR ENGINE SPECIFICATIONS

Engine	Disp. Cu. In.	Comp. Ratio	Bore X Stroke	Carbu-retion	Exhaust
425-Hp Turbo-Fire 409 V-8	409	11.0:1	4.313 x 3.50	Twin 4-bbl	Dual
400-Hp Turbo-Fire 409 V-8	409	11.0:1	4.313 x 3.50	4-bbl	Dual
300-Hp Turbo-Fire 327 V-8	409	10.0:1	4.313 x 3.50	4-bbl	Dual
250-Hp Turbo-Fire 327 V-8	327	10.5:1	4.00 x 3.25	4-bbl	Dual
340-Hp Turbo-Fire 409 V-8	327	10.5:1	4.00 x 3.25	4-bbl	Dual
230-Hp Turbo-Fire 327 V-8	327	8.6:1	4.00 x 3.25	4-bbl	Dual
195-Hp Turbo-Fire 283 V-8	283	9.25:1	3.875 x 3.0	2-bbl	Single
140-Hp Turbo-Fire 230 Six	230	8.5:1	3.875 x 3.25	1-bbl	Single

140-HP Turbo-Thrift 230 6 Cyl. Package
(Recommended for all-round utility work where outstanding economy is of prime importance.)
140-hp Turbo-Thrift 230 cu.-in. 6-cylinder engine.
Heavy-duty 3-Speed transmission (standard with all V-8s) and heavy-duty clutch
Heavy-duty battery, 70-ampere-hour
Heavy-duty front suspension ball joint assemblies
Stabilizer bar (standard on Station Wagon)
Heavy-duty brakes
Heavy-duty rear axle with roller-type wheel bearings
Special 3.36:1 axle ratio for Sedans

Special police-duty front and rear springs
Special police-duty front and rear shock absorbers
Deluxe steering wheel with horn ring
15 x 5.5K wheels with 6.70x15 tires
Speedometer calibrated to 2 percent accuracy, marked with 2-mph graduations
Heavy-duty front and rear seats
Thick foam pad for front seat
Heavy-duty floor mats with asphalt-impregnated pads
Instrument panel pad
Left-hand outside rearview mirror
Front seat belts for driver and passenger
Back-up Lights
Two-speed windshield wipers with push-button washer

195-Hp Turbo-Fire V-8 Package
(Recommended for urban patrol and cruising where a good balance of acceleration and economy is needed.)
195-hp Turbo-Fire 283 cu.-in. V-8 engine
3-Speed Synchro-Mesh transmission
Heavy-duty clutch
Heavy-duty battery, 70-ampere-hour rating
Heavy-duty front suspension ball joint assemblies
Heavy-duty brakes
Heavy-duty rear axle with roller-type wheel bearings
Special 3.36:1 axle ratio for Sedans, 3.55:1 for Station Wagons
Special police-duty front and rear springs
Special police-duty front and rear shock absorbers
Deluxe steering wheel with horn ring
15 x 5.5K wheels with 6.70x15 tires
Speedometer calibrated to 2 percent accuracy, marked with 2-mph graduations
Heavy-duty front and rear seats
Thick foam pad for front seat
Heavy-duty floor mats with asphalt-impregnated pads
Instrument panel pad
Left-hand outside rearview mirror
Front seat belts for driver and passenger
Back-up lights
Two-speed windshield wipers with push-button washer

230-Hp Turbo-Fire 327 V-8 Package
(Recommended for urban cruising and pursuit where peak performance on regular grade gasoline is called for.)
230-hp Turbo-Fire 327 cu.-in. V-8 engine
3-Speed Synchro-Mesh transmission
Heavy-duty radiator
Temperature-controlled fan
Heavy-duty battery, 70-ampere-hour rating
Heavy-duty front suspensioin ball joint assemblies
Heavy-duty brakes
Heavy-duty rear axle with roller-type wheel bearings
Special 3.55:1 axle ratio for Station Wagons
Special police-duty front and rear springs
Special police-duty front and rear shock absorbers
Deluxe steering wheel with horn ring
15 x 5.5K wheels with 6.70x15 tires
Speedometer calibrated to 2 percent accuracy, marked with 2-mph graduations
Heavy-duty front and rear seats
Thick foam pad for front sead
Heavy-duty floor mats with asphalt-impregnated pads
Instrument panel pad
Left-hand rearview mirror
Front seat belt for driver and passenger
Back-up lights
Two-speed windshield wipers with push-button washer

250-Hp Turbo-Fire 327 V-8 Package
(Recommended for highway cruising where excellent all-around performance is required.)
250-hp Turbo-Fire 327 cu.-in. V-8 engine
3-Speed Synchro-Mesh transmission
Heavy-duty radiator
Temperature-controlled fan
Heavy-duty battery, 70-ampere-hour rating
Heavy-duty front suspension ball joint assemblies
Heavy-duty brakes

Heavy-duty rear axle with roller-type wheel bearings
Special 3.55:1 axle ratio for Station Wagons
Special police-duty front and rear springs
Special police-duty front and rear shock absorbers
Deluxe steering wheel with horn ring
15 x 5.5K wheels with 6.70x15 tires
Speedometer calibrated to 2 percent accuracy, marked with 2-mph graduations
Heavy-duty front and rear seats
Thick foam pad for front seat
Heavy-duty floor mats with asphalt-impregnated pads
Instrument panel pad
Left-hand outside rearview mirror
Front seat belts for driver and passenger
Back-up lights
Two-speed windshield wipers with push-button washer

300-Hp Turbo-Fire 327 V-8 Package
(Recommended for highway cruising and pursuit where rapid acceleration and high performance are necessary.)
300-hp Turbo-Fire 327 cu.-in. V-8 engine
3-Speed Synchro-Mesh transmission
Heavy-duty radiator
Temperature-controlled fan
Heavy-duty battery, 70-ampere-hour rating
Heavy-duty front suspension ball joint assemblies
Heavy-duty brakes
Heavy-duty rear axle with roller-type wheel bearings
Special 3.55:1 axle ratio for Station Wagons
Special police-duty front and rear springs
Special police-duty front and rear shock absorbers
Deluxe steering wheel with horn ring
15 x 5.5K wheels with 6.70x15 tires
Speedometer calibrated to 2 percent accuracy, marked with 2-mph graduations
Heavy-duty front and rear seats
Thick foam pad for front seat
Heavy-duty floor mats with asphalt-impregnated pads
Instrument panel pad
Left-hand outside rearview mirror
Front seat belts for driver and passenger
Back-up lights
Two-speed windshield wipers with push-button washer

340-Hp Turbo-Fire 409 V-8 Package
(Recommended for high-speed highway pursuit where blistering acceleration and outstanding performance are vital.)
340-hp Turbo-Fire 409 cu.-in. V-8 engine
3-Speed Synchro-Mesh transmission
Heavy-duty radiator
Temperature-controlled fan
Heavy-duty battery, 70-ampere-hour rating
Heavy-duty front suspension ball joint assemblies
Heavy-duty brakes
Heavy-duty rear axle with roller-type wheel bearings
Special 3.55:1 axle ratio for Station Wagons
Special police-duty front and rear springs
Special police-duty front and rear shock absorbers
Deluxe steering wheel with horn ring
15 x 5.5K wheels with 6.70x15 tires
Speedometer calibrated to 2 percent accuracy, marked with 2-mph graduations
Heavy-duty front and rear seats
Thick foam pad for front seat
Heavy-duty floor mats with asphalt-impregnated pads
Instrument panel pad
Left-hand rearview mirror
Front seat belts for driver and passenger
Back-up lights
Two-speed windshield wipers with push-button washer

1980 CHEVROLET POLICE VEHICLES

Impala 9C1

An entirely new power lineup includes the new 3.8 Liter V-6 engine along with a 5.0 Liter 4-bbl. V-8 and a 5.7 Liter V-8 (available only to law enforcement agencies for law enforcement pursuit purposes.)

Standard Features

New side-lift frame jack lifts by the frame, not bumper, for greater convenience.
New door lock design helps make break-ins more difficult.
116-inch wheelbase with tight turning circle (38.8 feet curb-to-curb).
Interior hood release.
Window frame on doors of 4-door Sedan and Coupe.
Molded full foam seat construction.
Single-loop front seat and shoulder belt system.
New interior trim fabrics and colors.
Headlight dimmer switch on turn signal lever.
Three-speed automatic transmission.
Power steering.
Speedometer face includes metric numerals.
Built-in diagnostic connector for engine electrical system.
Delco Freedom battery never needs refilling.
High Energy Ignition System.
Power front disc/rear drum brake system with disc brake audible wear sensors.
Early Fuel Evaporation system.
Extensive corrosion-resistant treatments.

Malibu 9C1

The Chevy Malibu 9C1, with its mid-size 108.1-inch wheel-base, easy turning and maneuverability in city traffic, and generous overall interior room and trunk capacity. For 1980, there's a new, standard 3.8 Liter (229 cu. in.) 2-bbl. V-6. Available are a 5.0 Liter (305 cu. in.) 4-bbl. V-8 and a 5.7 Liter (350 cu. in.) 4-bbl. V-8 (available only to law enforcement agencies for law enforcement pursuit purposes).

Standard Features

108.1-in. wheelbase with tight turning circle (37.2 feet curb-to-curb).
All-welded, full-perimeter frame.
Window frame on doors of 4-door Sedan, with large fixed window in rear doors. Behind the rear windows are swing-out vents.
Extensive corrosion-resistant treatments.
High Energy Ignition.
Full Coil spring suspension.
Early Fuel Evaporation.
Coolant recovery system.
Power front disc/rear drum brakes with disc brake audible wear sensors.
Cushioned body mounting system.
Delco Freedom battery never needs refilling.
Single-loop seat and shoulder belt system.
Speedometer face includes metric numerals.
Interior hood release.
Vertically mounted spare tire.
Headlight dimmer switch on turn signal

1980 Impala Police Vehicle Powertrain Combinations

| Engines | | Displacement | | Carb | SAE NET Federal | | Axle Ratios Federal | | California | |
Option No.	Type	Liters	Cu. In.		HP @ RPM	Torque lb.-ft. @ RPM	Option	Ratio	Option	Ratio
RPO LC3	V-6	3.8	229	2-bbl	115 @ 4000	175 @ 2000	Base	2.73	—	—
RPO LG4	V-8	5.0	305	4-bbl	155 @ 4000 (155 @ 4000)	240 @ 1600 (230 @ 2400)	RPO G92	3.08	RPO YF5, G92	3.08
RPO LM1	V-8	5.7	350	4-bbl	165 @ 3800	260 @ 2400	Base	3.08	—	—

Dimensions		4-door Sedan	2-door Coupe
Exterior (Inches) Wheelbase		116.0	116.0
Overall Length		212.1	212.1
Wheel Tread:	Front	61.8	61.8
	Rear	60.8	60.8
Maximum Car Width		76.0	76.0
Overall Height (at design load)		56.0	55.3

9C1 POLICE VEHICLE EQUIPMENT

Higher gage frame.
Engine valve train durability features.
Greater capacity oil filter (1-quart capacity - V-8s only) (unavailable with 7P8 engine oil cooler).
Firm feel steering gear and linkage.
8.5-in. ring gear rear axle.
Temperature controlled fan on models without air conditioning.
Semi-metallic front brake pads.
11 x 2-in. 23 lb. rear brake drums.
Large bolt circle 15 x 7-in. wheels.
Special police pursuit suspension includes larger front and rear stabilizer bars, special springs and shocks (included only when police or QHK tires are ordered).
Larger radiator (same as RPO VO8).
Fuel vapor return system on V-8s.
Special balanced drive shaft.

276

1980 Malibu Police Vehicle Powertrain Combinations

| Engines | | Displacement | | Carb | SAE NET Federal | | Axle Ratios | | | |
| Option No. | Type | Liters | Cu. In. | | HP @ RPM | Torque lb.-ft. @ RPM | Federal | | California | |
							Option	Ratio	Option	Ratio
RPO LC3	V-6	3.8	229	2-bbl	115 @ 4000	175 @ 2000	Base	2.41	—	—
RPO LG4	V-8	5.0	305	4-bbl	155 @ 4000 (155 @ 4000)	240 @ 1600 (230 @ 2400)	RPO G92	2.73	RPO G92 & YF5	2.73
RPO LM1	V-8	5.7	350	4-bbl	165 @ 3800	260 @ 2400	Base	2.73	—	—

Dimensions		4-door Sedan	2-door Coupe
Exterior (Inches) Wheelbase		108.1	108.1
Overall Length		192.7	192.7
Wheel Tread:	Front	58.5	58.5
	Rear	57.8	57.8
Maximum Car Width		71.5	71.5
Overall Height (at design load)		54.2	53.3

9C1 POLICE VEHICLE EQUIPMENT

Higher gage frame.

Engine valve train durability features.

Greater capacity oil filter (1-quart capacity on V8s only) (unavailable with 7P8 engine oil cooler).

Front and rear semi-metallic brake linings.

Vented, higher gage wheels 14 x 6-in. 5-bolt.

Specific body mounts.

Special police suspension includes front and rear stabilizer bars, special springs and shocks, special front suspension jounce bumpers (only when QFK tires or pursuit tires are ordered).

Higher cooling capacity radiator (same as RPO VO8).

Temperature controlled fan on models without air conditioning.

Fuel vapor return system on V-8s.

Special balanced drive shaft.

Specific brake master cylinder and booster.

1994 CAPRICE POLICE PACKAGE

Caprice Classic Model 1BL19

Standard Equipment:
4.3 Liter V-8 engine with SFI
4-Speed automatic overdrive transmission
Air Conditioning with environmentally friendly refrigerant
All-season steel-belted radial ply tires (P215/75R-15 blackwall)
Base-coat/clear-coat paint
Body-side moldings
Brakes: Four-wheel anti-lock brake system ABS (front disc / rear drum)
Child security rear door locks
Cloth bench seats with front center armrest
Comfortilt steering wheel
Brake transmission interlock
Composite halogen headlamps
Driver and passenger side (air bag) Supplemental Inflatable restraint system, manual lap / shoulder safety belts for all outboard seating positions; manual lap safety belts, center seating positions.
Dual outside rearview mirrors (LH remote)
Electric digital speedometer with trip odometer and gauges
Oil change monitor
Full Frame
Full Wheel Covers
Headlamps-on reminder tone
Intermittent windshield wipers
Power Steering
Stainless steel exhaust
15 x 17-in. steel wheels
AM/F stereo with seek-scan, digital clock, dual front door mounted and dual rear mounted speakers
Tinted Glass
Wet-arm windshield washer system
Pass-Key Theft Deterrent (N/A with Police Package)

Caprice Classic 'LS' Model 1BN19
(The following equipment is in addition to or replacing items included in the standard equipment summary.)
15 x 7-in. Aluminum Wheels (HD steel wheels and wire wheel covers required with police package)
Cloth 55/45 split seat with armrest
Power Driver Seat
Electronic Speed Control
Deluxe interior trim including trunk
Door-mounted courtesy lamps
Dual reading lamps in rear-view mirror includes rear seat reading lamps
"Caprice Classic LS" exterior emblems
Body side pin striping
Power door locks
Power windows with driver express down and passenger window lock-out switch
AM/FM stereo with seek-scan, stereo cassette tape player with auto reverse, Extended Range Sound System, and digital clock
Luggage compartment area hold-down net
Power Dual Electronic outside mirrors
Power Trunk Opener

Caprice Classic Police Package

9C1 Features
Heavy-duty full perimeter frame
8.5-in. ring gear rear axle
Special Police Pursuit Suspension includes front and rear stabilizer bars, special springs and shocks, firm-feel steering, and specific body mounts
Tires, P225/70R15 SBR Blackwell "Speed Rated" All Season with full size spare tire.
Semi-metallic front and rear disc brake linings with larger rear wheel cylinders
Cooling Package, includes higher wattage dual electric fans, transmission oil cooler integral with radiator and heavy duty condenser.
Engine oil cooler (external)

Power steering fluid cooler (external)

Delcotron 140 amp Alternator (See page 17 for specifications)

Maintenance Free 770 CCA heavy-duty battery (See page 7 for specifications)

Special calibrated transmission (use overdrive for high speed driving)

Air Conditioning wide open throttle cut-off

Air Conditioning head pressure relief

Transmission Low Gear Blockout (prevents manual downshift to first gear)

Wiring Provision for Headlamp Flashing Unit (also used with Option 6J3)

Special Balanced Driveshaft

Hoses-silicon radiator and heater includes worm drive hose clamps

Digital Speedometer Certified 1 MPH increments 0 to 199 MPH, includes: Trip Odometer, Gauges (Oil, Temp, Volts) plus Warning Lights and Speedometer light off switch

Anti-Corrosion Hot Melt Pads under front and rear floor insulators

Radio Bonding Strap Package

Wiring Provision for Horn/Siren Circuit Connection (also used with Option 6J4)

Auxiliary Junction Block in engine compartment

Trunk Opener, electric left-side of steering column near headlight switch

Single Key Locking System - random key code for each vehicle, one key operates ignition and all other locks.

Heavy-duty bench seats with front seat armrest-cloth trim

Auxiliary Fuse Block provides six additional fused circuits at 20 amps each

15 x 7 H/D Steel Wheels

Bolt on center hubcaps

Caprice Classic Police Package Powertrain Combinations

Engines	Type	Displacement Liters/Cu.In.	Engine Fuel System	Transmission	Axle Ratio
L99 Standard Single Exhaust	V-8	4.3/265	Sequential Fuel Injection	MXO 4L60E Electric 4-Speed Auto w/OD	3.23
L99 Optional Bi-Fuel KL6	V-8	4.3/265	Primary Natural Gas Secondary Gas	MXO 4L60E Electric 4-Speed Auto w/OD	3.23
LT1 Optional Dual Exhaust	V-8	5.7/350	Sequential Fuel Injection	MXO 4L60E Electric 4-Speed Auto w/OD	3.08)

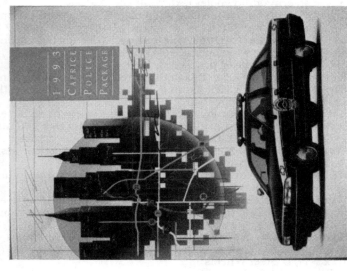

1994 Specifications and Dimensions
(Dimensions are in inches unless otherwise specified.)

General		Engine (STD. - OPT.)	(L99) V-8	(LT1) V-8
Wheelbase:	115.9	Type:		
Overall Length:	214.1	Displacement Liters (cu.in.)	4.3 (265)	5.7 (350)
Overall width:	77.0			
Overall height:	55.7	Horsepower/RPM:	200 @ 5200	260 @ 5000
Tread Front:	61.8	Torque/RPM:	245 @ 2400	330 @ 3200
Tread Rear:	62.3)	Induction System:	SFI	SFI
Fuel Tank Capacity:	23.0 gals.	Compression Ratio:	9.9:1	10.0:1
Aerodynamics: Coefficient of drag	.34	Exhaust:	Single	Dual

1994 CAMARO POLICE VEHICLE

Camaro 2-door Hatchback (1FP87) Preferred Equipment Group FCAB

Standard Features
Driver's Side 4-Way Manual Seat Adjuster
Closeout Panel For Cargo Compartment Area
Dual Reading/Courtesy Lamps in ISRV Mirror
Vanity Visor Mirros, Covered, Driver and Passenger
Tinted Glass
Solar Control Glass
4-Wheel Anti Lock Brake system
Front Disc and Rear Drum Power Brakes
Stainless Steel Exhaust System
Brake Transmission Shift Interlock (Automatic Only)
Miniquad Halogen Headlamps
PASS-Key II Theft Deterrent System
Air Bag System, Driver and Passenger
3-Point Safety Belts for All Seating Positions
Base-Coat/Clear-Coat Exterior Finish
Black Dual Sport Mirrors (L.H. Remote, R.H. Manual)
Intermittent Wiper System
Full Floor Carpeting
Carpeted Cargo Area
Front Floor Mats
Center Console with Cup Holder and Lighted Storage Console
Power Rack & Pinion Steering
4-Wheel Coil Spring Suspension System with Computer-Selected Springs
Short-Long Arm (SLA) Front Suspension System
Front and Rear Stabilizer Bars
Single Serpentine Belt Accessory Drive
Compact High Pressure Spare Tire
Energy-Absorbing Front and Rear Bumpers with Body-Color Fascias
Side Window Defoggers
Comfortilt Steering Wheel
Scotchgard Fabric Protector-Seats, Door Trim, Floor Carpeting and Front Floor Mats
Locking Glovebox, Lighted
Integral Rear Spoiler
Storage Compartment in Doors
AM/FM Stereo Radio w/Seek-Scan, Stereo Cassette Tape w/Search-Repeat and Digital Clock

Special Service Package B4C

Standard Features
5.7 Liter engine
6-Speed manual transmission
Dual exhaust outlets
16-in. aluminum wheels
P245/50ZR16 BW tires
Four wheel disc brakes
Engine oil cooler
Transmission oil cooler (automatic only)
Alternator 140 amp (50 amps at idle)
Speedometer to 150 mph (1 mph increments) with gauges and trip odometer
Air conditioning
Battery 525CCA (90 minutes reserve capacity)
Performance suspension for ride and handling

Camaro Special Service Package B4C Powertrain Combinations

Engine Code	Type	Displacement Liters/Cu. In.	Engine Fuel System	Transmission Code	Type	Axle Ratio
LT1	V-8	5.7/350	Sequential Fuel Injection	MN6 6-Speed Manual, w/OD	MM6	3.42 Limited Slip
LT1	V-8	5.7/350	Sequential Fuel Injection	MXO 4-Speed Auto, w/OD (Optional)	4L60E	3.23 Limited Slip

1994 Specifications and Dimensions
(Dimensions are in inches unless otherwise specified.)

General	
Wheelbase:	101.1
Overall Length:	193.2
Overall width:	74.1
Overall height:	51.3
Tread Front:	60.7
Tread Rear:	60.6
Fuel Tank Capacity:	15.5 gals.
Aerodynamics: Coefficient of drag	.338

Engine	
Type:	V-8
Displacement Liters (cu.in.)	5.7 (350)
Horsepower/RPM:	275 @ 5000
Torque/RPM:	325 @ 2400
Induction System:	SFI
Compression Ratio:	10.5:1
Exhaust:	Dual

Chassis	
Frame:	Full Unitized Steel
Front Suspension:	Independent - SLA, Coil Steel Alloy Spring, Steel Anti-Roll Bar, Gas Charged Shocks
Rear Suspension:	Salisbury 4-Link, Coil Steel Alloy Spring, Steel Anti-Roller Bar, Gas Charged Shocks
Steering Type:	Power Rack & Pinion
Steering Ratio:	14.4:1

1959 FORD POLICE CARS

Ford 300-hp Police Interceptor 352 Special V-8 (available only to law enforcement agencies)

POLICE INTERCEPTOR V-8 PACKAGE includes the following chassis components: Heavy-duty front and rear springs; heavy-duty front and rear shock absorbers; heavy-duty rear axle assembly with higher capacity drive pinion bearings, axle shafts and wheel bearings; heavy-duty front and rear riveted brake linings (lining area is increased to 203 sq. in. and drums are specially ribbed for better cooling, surer braking and longer lining life); 65 amp-hour battery when automatic transmission is selected; plus extra cooling capacity radiator.

Four quick-responding transmissions to select from

CRUISE-O-MATIC DRIVE
Offers a choice of 2 full-time driving ranges: "D1" -- used for all normal driving -- gives brisk, solid take-offs in low; "D2" gives gentle, sure-footed intermediate starts on wet, icy or loose surfaces. With the Police Interceptor 352 Special V-8, you get a special 3.10 rear axle ratio for outstanding high performance.

NEW FORDOMATIC DRIVE
Brand-new lighter weight, simplified design utilizes a single-stage, 3-element torque converter and a compound planetary gear set with only one clutch assembly that provides two forward gear ratios (low and drive), plus reverse. Starts the car in low for smooth, instant responding, lively getaways. Normally needs no periodic service.

ECONOMICAL OVERDRIVE
Delivers more miles per gallon, saves on engine wear and permits quieter driving. Economical automatic 4th gear lets the engine purr along at about 28 percent lower rpm than required at the same road speed in direct gear, for really smooth "cruising." Has a "kick down" into direct (by flooring accelerator) for fast pickup.

HIGH-TORQUE CONVENTIONAL
Provides 3 manual-shift forward speeds and a reverse. Has a semi-centrifugal, cushion-disc type, high-torque transmitting clutch. Features rugged, all helical gears with synchronizers for extra long life. Advance-design linkage provides easy shifting into all gears, smoothly and quietly.

Highlight Features
- New Super-fitted aluminum alloy pistons have longer skirts for better oil control
- New standard vacuum-booster type fuel pump for more positive windshield-wiper action
- Electronically mass-balanced under own power for factory-tested optimum smoothness
- High-velocity, low-silhouette 4-barrel carburetor for most versatile, most economical operation regardless of driving conditions
- Zero-lash, hydraulic valve lifters provide more accurate valve functioning for optimum performance, quieter operation
- Full-pressure lubrication with fully disposable Full-Flow Oil Filter for surest engine protection, handiest filter changing
- Large intake and exhaust valves and ports for freer breathing, higher performance, greater economy
- Super-Filter air cleaner for maximum engine protection, easier, more economical maintenance
- Turbo-Action, gasketless 18mm. spark plugs have long central core for greater self-cleansing action, more uniform combustion, better operating temperature control for greater economy

225-hp THUNDERBIRD 332 Special V-8
This distinguished member of the Thunderbird V-8 family features Ford's Precision Fuel Induction system. Has high-velocity 2-barrel carburetor, and wedge-shaped combustion chambers for instant-responding performance in any kind of going. Short-stroke, low-friction design for economy and long life. New standard vacuum-booster fuel pump provides positive windshield-wiper operation. Full-pressure lubrication with disposable Full-Flow Oil Filter. Sturdy Deep-Block Construction for long life.

200-hp FORD THUNDERBIRD 292 V-8
Ford's Thunderbird 292-cu. in. V-8 engine for '59 offers high-compression, high-torque performance for quick getaways and agile response in traffic.
It has a higher-velocity 2-barrel carburetor with greater gas-saving efficiency on regular gasoline, new high-pressure vacuum-booster type fuel pump, new positive engine ventilation, plus all of Ford's time-proven features for durability and economy. Like all Ford V-8 engines, it is electronically balanced under its own power for optimum smoothness.

145-hp MILEAGE MAKER SIX

Features Ford's Deep-Block Design: high-compression, high-turbulance, wedge-shaped combustion chambers; new vacuum-booster fuel pump; angle-mounted Super-Filter air cleaner; unit-design carburetor for top mileage on regular fuel; plus other advances. (Available on all models with Conventional, Overdrive and new Fordomatic transmissions.)

1959 FORD POLICE CAR SPECIFICATIONS

Clutch and Manual Transmissions: Semi-centrifugal clutch with full-weighted levers for positive engagement, suspended clutch pedal; 9-1\2-in. dia. with Six, 10-in. dia. with Thunderbird 292 V-8, and 11-in. dia. with Police Interceptor and Thunderbird Special V-8 engines. Conventional Drive has 3 forward speeds and 1 reverse, with gear ratios tailored to each engine. Shot-peened, fine-pitch helical gears for high strength and quietness; forged bronze-synchronizers. Overdrive (optional) is combination of 3-speed transmission plus an automatic 4th gear that cuts in at about 28 mph, cuts out at about 22 mph.

Automatic Drive (optional): New Fordomatic has a single-stage 3-element torque converter and compound planetary gear set with only one clutch assembly that provides two "forward" gears (low and direct), plus reverse. Contained in lightweight, cast aluminum housing. Water-cooled with all engines (not available with Police Interceptor V-8). Cruise-O-Matic -- offers low-gear stars in "D1" range for full-power getaways, and intermediate-gear starts in "D2" range for sure-footed acceleration. With Police Interceptor and Thunderbird Special V-8 only.

Wide-Contoured Frame: 5-cross-member, precision-made, reinforced box-section construction. Side rails extend outside passenger seating area for better foot room and increased side protection. Silent-Grip body mounting system.

Front Suspension: Swept-Back, Angle-Poised, Ball-Joint Front Suspension has new link-type rubber-bushed stabilizer, plus threaded, permanently lubricated bushings in upper control arm for soft, easy ride. Viscous-control shock absorbers.

Rear Suspension: Soft-action, variable-rate type, out-board-mounted, long-leaved rear springs with extra leaf lengths ahead of axle for smooth, comfortable Even-Kneel ride. 4 leaves on Custom 300 and Fairlane, 6 leaves on station wagons, with new plastic-type, graphite-impregnated friction control inserts. Fully insulated with rubber bushings in front and rear eyes. Tension-type shackles. Wind-up rubber bumper on frame side rail over forward spring section limits deflection under load, further contributing to Even-Keel ride. Newly valved, Viscous-control shock absorbers.

Steering: Magic-Circle recirculating-ball type steering gear provides low friction, easy steering. Antifriction bearings throughout. Symmetrical-linkage; 27:1 overall ratio; 17-1\2-in. 3-spoke (Lifeguard deep-dish steering wheel. Approx. 20-ft. turning radius.

Brakes: Giant-Grip, Double-Sealed, self-energizing hydraulic; suspended pedal; 11-in. dia. drum; 180-sq. in. lining area on Custom 300 and Fairlane, 191-sq. in. on station wagons.

1959 Engine Specifications And Availability

ENGINE	HP	TORQUE	CARB.	BORE & STROKE	EXH.	RATIO	DISP. CU. IN.	TRANSMISSION	MODELS
Police Interceptor 352 Special V-8	300	380 lb-ft	Four-barrel	4.00" x 3.50"	Dual	9.6:1	352	Conventional Overdrive Cruise-O-Matic	Custom 300 Fairlane Station Wagons
Thunderbird 332 Special V-8	225	325 lb-ft	Two-barrel	4.00" x 3.30"	Single	8.9:1	332	Cruise-O-Matic Fordomatic	Custom 300 Fairlane Station Wagons
Thunderbird 292 V-8	200	285 lb-ft	Two-barrel	3.75" x 3.30"	Single	8.8:1	292	Conventional Overdrive Fordomatic	Custom 300 Fairlane Station Wagons
Mileage Maker Six	145	206 lb-ft	Single-barrel	3.62" x 3.60"	Single	8.4:1	223	Conventional Overdrive Fordomatic	Custom 300 Fairlane Station Wagons

1964 Ford Police Cars

FORD CUSTOM AND FORD CUSTOM 500 SERIES POLICE CARS

Ford Police Cars offer new Custom and Custom 500 Series -- 20 cars in all -- a choice of 2- or 4-door models in five power ranges: the 33-hp Police Interceptor, power-packed for outstanding acceleration and sustained high speeds of freeway patrol; the 300-hp Police Cruiser, V-8 powered for rugged highway operation; the Police Guardian, with 250-hp V-8, excels in city and highway patrol; the Police Sentinel, tops in routine police work, has a new 195-hp V-8; the Police Deputy with the 138-hp Police Special Six for economical utility operation.

'64 FORD POLICE INTERCEPTOR
POWERED BY THE MIGHTY INTERCEPTOR 4V/390 V-8
Displacement - 390 cu.in.
Horsepower - 330 @ 5000
Torque (lb-ft) @ rpm - 427 @ 3200
Compression Ratio - 10.1:1
Carburetor - 4-venturi
Fuel - premium
Alternator - Single Belt Drive - 42 amp.
Transmission - Axle Ratios:
3- or 4-Speed Manual or Overdrive - 3.50:1
(opt.) 4.11:1
Interceptor Cruise-O-Matic 3.00:1
(opt.) 3.50:1

Equipment Included In Police Interceptor Package:
330-hp Police Interceptor 4V/390 V-8
11-Inch Clutch
70 Amp-Hr HD Battery

Plus:
Manual 3-Speed Fully Synchronized Transmission
Hi-Speed and Handling Package, Includes HD Springs with HD Extra-Control Shock Absorbers, Front and Rear, and HD Front Stabilizer Bar
Reinforced Mono-Pivot Front Lower Suspension Arms
HD Fade-Resistant Brakes with Riveted Linings, Manual Adjustment
HD Maximum Head Room, Full Width Front Seat and Padding (formed foam front and blanket foam rear padded cushions)
Extra-Cooling Radiator
Certified Calibration Speedometer (2 mph increments)
HD Floor Mats, Black Rubber, Front and Rear

Highly Recommended Options
Interceptor Cruise-O-Matic Transmission (LPO)
Front Seat Belts for Driver and Passenger (RPO)
Padded Instrument Panel and Two Cushioned Sun Visors (RPO)
15" Tires and Wheels Required (LPO)

'64 POLICE CRUISER

The Police Cruiser is recommended where high power is desirable, but Interceptor peak performance is not required. Both models are identical in everything except engines. The Cruiser is powered by the rugged 300-hp Thunderbird 4V/390 V-8, which has acceleration characteristics similar to the Interceptor's. Package equipment and most recommended options are same for both except for engine and regular Cruise-O-Matic transmission.

THUNDERBIRD 4V/390 V-8
Displacement - 390 cu. in.
Horsepower @ rpm - 300 @ 4600
Torque (lb-ft) @ rpm - 427 @ 2800
Compression Ratio - 10.1:1
Carburetor - 4-venturi

Fuel - premium
Transmission - Axle Ratios:
3- or 4-Speed Manual or Overdrive - 3.50:1
(opt.) - 3.89:1
Cruise-O-Matic - 3.00:1
(opt.) - 3.50:1

1964 Ford Police Car Specifications
CLUTCHES AND TRANSMISSIONS: Heavy-Duty Clutches in Police Packages have extra-thick facings, pressure-lube fitting on release bearing, needle-roller bearings in release lever fulcrum points, and extra-capacity pressure-plate springs. All are semi-centrifugal type. Face diameter and frictional area is: 11-in. (113.1 sq. in.) with 390 and 352 V-8s; 10.4-in. (103.5 sq. in.) with 289 V-8, 11-in. (123.7 sq. in.) with Six, Standard sedan clutch face diameter and frictional area: 11-in. (113.1 sq. in.) with 390 and 352 V-8s; 10.4-in. (101.9 sq. in.) with 289 V-8; 9-1\2-in. (85.22 sq. in.) with Six, 3-Speed Manual Transmission (standard all engines) is fully synchronized in all for-

ward speeds, with hardened and shot-peened alloy-steel helical gears, and forged bronze synchronizers. 4-Speed Manual Transmission (optional for 390 V-8s) is fully synchronized in all forward speeds, with floor-mounted shift lever. Overdrive (optional except with 352 V-8) has 3-speed manual transmission plus automatic 4th gear that cuts in above 28 mph and cuts out below 21 mph (approx.), with downshift for passing by flooring accelerator. Lockout control on instrument panel. Cruise-O-Matic Transmission (optional all engines) is 3-speed automatic transmission with dual range drive selection; three-speed range starting in low for all normal driving, or two-speed range starting in intermediate for gradual acceleration on slippery surfaces. Vacuum-controlled transmission throttle valve. Interceptor Cruise-O-Matic is specially calibrated for faster upshift at higher rpm.

REAR AXLE: Police Package heavy-duty axles on sedans (standard on wagons) are semi-floating type with deep-offset hypoid gears and straddle-mounted drive pinion. Also included, with fade- or wear-resistant brakes, are higher capacity wheel bearings and large diameter axle shafts.

ELECTRICAL: 12-volt electrical system with 30-amp generator. Police Package has 66-plate, 70 amp-hour battery (78-plate, 65 amp-hour in Sentinel). Standard sedan has 66-plate, 55 amp-hour battery. Weatherproof ignition system with Static-Ban constant resistance wiring and air-cooled distributor points; 18mm Turbo-Action spark plugs; inertia-engagement starter.

SUSPENSION: Police Package has reinforced mono-pivot lower front suspension arms with lube fittings on upper inner arm bushings, plus heavy-duty coil springs, shock absorbers, and front stabilizer bar. Rear-Asymmetrical, variable-rate design with rear axle located well forward from center of springs for anti-dive and anti-squat on braking and acceleration. Extra-long, gentle-rate, leaf-type springs with wide spring base for stable, levelized ride. Tension-type shackles. Diagonally mounted shock absorbers. Police Package has heavy-duty springs and shock absorbers.

STEERING: Precision-control, low-friction recirculating ball type steering gear with anti-friction bearings throughout plus high ratio for easier steering. Flexible coupling in steering shaft insulates steering wheel. Symmetrical linkage with nylon bearings in tie rod and pitman arm pivots packed with special 36,000-mile or 3-year grease retained by full-life seals. Over-all steering ratio 30 to 1; with power steering 23 to 1. Turning diameter 41 feet.

BRAKES: Hydraulic, double-sealed, self-energizing design. Dash-mounted master cylinder. Police Package heavy-duty brakes have 234-sq. in. riveted linings (bonded on Deputy) and specially grooved 11-in. dia. composite drums for maximum cooling and fade resistance. Manual adjustment. Standard sedan brakes have 212-sq. in. (234-sq. in. on Wagons) riveted linings, air-grooved 11-in. composite drums in self-adjustment. Foot-operated parking brake with hand release under instrument panel. Swift Sure power brakes with special low pedal are optional.

1978 FORD LTD POLICE CARS

Ideally suited for a variety of patrol service applications, the LTD police unit is equipped with a broad spectrum of standard equipment features. Notable items include power steering, power front disc brakes, Cruise-O-Matic transmission, "Police Radial" tires, front bumper guards, power ventilation system and a large bin-type glove box.

Ford also has expanded its line-up for 1978 to include five engine packages. You can choose the power team best suited to meet your requirements. From the economy-oriented 5.0 litre (302 cu. in. 2V V-8 engine, to the high performance 7.5 litre (460 cu. in. Interceptor. The 1978 Ford LTD can be equipped to handle many police applications.

Ford Police Packages are available on LTD 2-door and 4-door Pillared Hardtops, and LTD Station Wagon models. The five extra-duty packages provide a wide selection for a variety of patrol and pursuit assignments.

THE 5.0 LITRE PACKAGE provides departments with the benefits of a full-size car with the thrifty 5.0 litre (302 cu. in. 2V V-8 engine. The 5.0 Litre Package is ideal for light duty police work, such as personnel transport and routine investigations, where quick acceleration is not required.

THE 5.8 LITRE PACKAGE suited for a multitude of duty assignments is equipped with the 5.8 Litre (351 CU. IN.) 2V V-8 engine for brisk performance. The engine features cooper-lead alloy bearings, free turn valves and hydraulic lifters.

THE 6.6 LITRE PACKAGE includes the popular 6.6 litre (400 CU. IN.) 2V V-8 engine. This engine is a long stroke engine with square bore and stroke. Designed for all-around patrol duty, the 6.6 Litre Package is especially suited for city and suburban cruising.

THE 7.5 LITRE PACKAGE is built around the high performance 7.5 litre (460 CU. IN.) 4V V-8 engine, and is designed for quick acceleration and fast maneuverability in suburban areas. The 7.5 Litre Package is second only to the Police Interceptor in total performance.

THE 7.5 LITRE INTERCEPTOR PACKAGE, equipped with the 7.5 litre (460 CU. IN.) 4V V-8 engine, is a maximum duty package capable of continued high speed required for highway and freeway pursuit. The 7.5 Litre P.I. engine features a specially balanced crankshaft that is balanced at higher rpm than regular engines. It also includes heavy-duty bearings, heavy-duty oil pump and hardened exhaust valve seats. Extra performance also has been provided through the use of a high-capacity air cleaner and low restriction dual exhaust.

1978 Ford Power Team Data

Feature	LTD				LTD II			
	5.0 Litre (302 CU. IN.) Police	5.8 Litre (351 CU. IN.) Police	6.6 Litre (400 CU. IN.) Police	7.5 Litre (460 CU. IN.) Police	7.5 Litre (460 CU. IN.) Interceptor	5.0 Litre (302 CU. IN.) Police	5.8 Litre (351 CU. IN.) Police	6.6 Litre (400 CU. IN.) Police
Displacement (litres)	5.0 (302 CU. IN.) 2V V-8	5.8 (351 CU. IN.) 2V V-8	6.6 (400 CU. IN.) 2V V-8	7.5 (460 CU. IN.) 4V V-8	7.5 (460 CU. IN.) 4V V-8	5.0 (302 CU. IN.) 2V V-8	5.8 (351 CU. IN.) 2V V-8	6.6 (400 CU. IN.) 2V V-8
Alternator	70-amp	70-amp	70-amp	70-amp	90-amp	70-amp	70-amp	70-amp
Trans	Auto.	Auto.	Auto.	Auto.	Auto. H-D	Auto.	Auto.	Auto.
Battery (amp-hour)	77	77	77	77	77	77	77	77
Rear Axle Ratio	2.75:1	2.50:1	3.00:1	2.75:1	3.00:1	2.75:1	2.50:1	3.00:1

1978 Ford LTD Police Packages	5.0 LITRE PACKAGE	5.8 LITRE PACKAGE	6.6 LITRE PACKAGE	7.5 LITRE PACKAGE	7.5 LITRE INTERCEPTOR PACKAGE
Engine Displacement (litre)	5.0	5.8	6.6	7.5	7.5
Alternator - 70 Ampere - 90 Ampere	Std. Opt.	Std. Opt.	Std. Opt.	Std. Opt.	N.A. Std.
Solid State DuraSpark Ignition	Std.	Std.	Std.	Std.	Std.
Transistorized Voltage Regulator	Std.	Std.	Std.	Std.	Std.
Heavy-Duty Battery - 77 Ampere	Std.	Std.	Std.	Std.	Std.
Engine Lubricating Oil Cooler	N.A.	N.A.	N.A.	N.A.	Std.
Coolant Recovery System	Std.	Std.	Std.	Std.	Std.
Extra Cooling Package - Includes extra-fin density radiator and shrouded flex-blade fan that adjusts automatically to demand.	Std.	Std.	Std.	Std.	Std.
Automatic Transmission with First-Gear Lock-Out and Auxiliary Oil Cooler	Std.	Std.	Std.	Std.	N.A.
Special Interceptor heavy-duty Cruise-O-Matic Transmission with Auxiliary Oil Cooler and First Gear Lock-Out	N.A.	N.A.	N.A.	N.A.	Std.
First Gear Lock-Out Delete	Opt.	Opt.	Opt.	Opt.	Opt.
Rear Axle Ratios	2.75:1	2.50:1	3.00:1	2.75:1	3.00:1
Clutch Blade Fan	N.A.	N.A.	N.A.	Std.	Std.
Exhaust System	Single	Single	Single	Single	Dual
Low Restriction Air Cleaner and Dual Exhaust System	N.A.	N.A.	N.A.	N.A.	Std.
Power Front Disc/Rear Drum Brakes with Organic Linings	Std.	Std.	Std.	N.A.	N.A.

1978 Ford LTD Police Packages	5.0 LITRE PACKAGE	5.8 LITRE PACKAGE	6.6 LITRE PACKAGE	7.5 LITRE PACKAGE	7.5 LITRE INTERCEPTOR PACKAGE
Heavy-Duty Police Power Front Disc/Rear Drum Brakes with Semi-metallic Heavy-Duty Front Disc Pads, Heavy-Duty Rear Linings and Flared Grooved Rear Drums	N.A.	Opt.	Opt.	Std.	Std.
Power Steering with Forward Mounted Fluid Cooler	Std.	Std.	Std.	Std.	Std
Police Maximum Handling Packages - Includes Extra Heavy-Duty, High-Rate Front and Rear Springs, Extra-Control Shock Absorbers, Heavy-Duty Front and Rear Police Stabilizer Bars, Rear Track Bar, Rear Lower Suspension Arm Bushings and Heavy-Duty Front Drag Strut Insulator (Rear Stabilizer Bar Not Available on Wagon Models)	Std.	Std.	Std.	Std.	Std.
Split Float Carburetor	N.A.	N.A.	N.A.	N.A.	Std.
High Performance Camshaft	N.A.	N.A.	N.A.	N.A.	Std.
Electrical Fuel Pump	N.A.	N.A.	N.A.	N.A.	Std.
Heavy-Duty 15 x 6.5 inch Safety Rim Wheels	Std.	Std.	Std.	Std.	Std.
Heavy-Duty Front Seat	Std.	Std.	Std.	Std.	Std.
Calibrated Speedometer, (0-140) in 2 MPH increments - Kilometer/MPH graphics	Std.	Std.	Std.	Std.	Std.
Automatic Parking Brake Release	Std.	Std.	Std.	Std.	Std.
Dual Beam Map Light	Std.	Std.	Std.	Std.	Std.
Remote Control Electric Trunk Lid Release in Glove Box	Std.	Std.	Std.	Std.	Std.
HR70x15 BSW "Police Radial" Tires (non-steel) - N.A. on Wagons	Std.	Std.	Std.	Std.	Std.
JR78x15 BSW "Police Radial" Tires (non-steel) - Standard on Wagons	Opt.	Opt.	Opt.	Opt.	Opt.
JR70x15 BSW/WSW "Police Radial" Tires (non-steel)	Opt.	Opt.	Opt.	Opt.	Opt.

1993 FORD MUSTANG SPECIAL SERVICE PACKAGE

Standard Features
Speedometer head assembly - certified calibration 0 to 160 mph in 2 mph increments
Air deflector, front lower radiator
Axle, Traction-Lok 8.8-inch
Alternator, 75-amp
Battery, 58-amp, maintenance-free, heavy-duty (540 CCA) with 100 minute reserve capacity
Brakes, power disc front/drum rear w/metal disc brake rotor shields
Engine, 5.0L HO V-8 with sequential multi-port fuel injection
Engine Oil Cooler
Exhaust System, dual with stainless tailpipe terminations
Front floor pan, reinforced both sides
Fuel tank capacity - 15.4 gallons
Hose clamps, aircraft - type radiator and heater
Moldings, body-color bodyside protection
Oil cooler, automatic transmission - external front-mounted
Spare tire and wheel - conventional
Stabilizer bars, front (1.3-in. dia.)/rear (.83-in. dia.)
Steering, power rack-and-pinion with increased effort
Suspension, modified MacPherson strut with stabilizer bar front and variable-rate coil springs; front-bar-link and quadra-shock rear
Tires, P215/65R15 95V BSW, all-season performance Goodyear Eagle GT+4
    Transmission,5-speed manual overdrive
Wheels, 15 x 7-in. cast aluminum, 10-hole

Available Options
Law Enforcement Modifications
VASCAR speedometer cable, 2-piece
Radio noise suppression (RR) package - police radio
Alternator, 130-amp
Hoses, silicone with special hose clamps (water bypass available)
Molding delete, front doors only
Seats - Heavy-duty bucket, reclining, low-back cloth with head restraints (replaces articulated sports seats-mandatory with Special Service Package)
Tires, P225/55ZR16 BSW performance unidirectional (not applicable with Special Service Package)
Transmission, 4-speed automatic overdrive

Engine
5.0L (302 cu. in.) High Output Sequential multi-port electronic fuel injection with EEC-IV electric engine controls

Transmissions
5-speed manual overdrive - standard
4-speed automatic overdrive - optional
Axle ratio: 3.08 (manual); 2.73 (automatic)

Horsepower and Torque Ratings
Horsepower: 205 net @ 4200 rpm
    Torque: 270 lb.-ft. net @ 3000 rpm

'93 Mustang Police Specifications And Dimension

Wheelbase:		100.5"
Overall Length:		179.6"
Overall height:		52.1"
Overall width:		68.3"
Tread:	Front:	57.9"
	Rear:	57.0"
Base model curb weight		2,834 lbs.

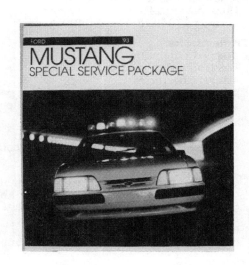

1993 FORD CROWN VICTORIA INTERCEPTOR POLICE PACKAGE

Standard Features

Electronic speedometer, certified calibration in 2 mph increments, 0 to 140 mpg
Bodyside molding delete, front door (molding shipped in trunk)
Air dam, lower radiator
Alternator, 130 amp.
Axle ratio, rear 3.27:1
Battery, 4-wheel disc, police level, with metal front dust shields
Cooling Package, police level, with 8-blade plastic fan
Drive shaft and U-joints, heavy-duty
Engine, 4.6L with police pursuit calibration
Exhaust system, stainless steel, dual
Frame mounts, heavy-duty
Ignition system, distributorless
Power steering, speed-sensitive, variable assist
Power steering oil cooler, front-mounted
Suspension, police, heavy-duty front and rear springs shock absorbers and stabilizer bars
Tires, P225/70HR15 BSW, all-season speed rated with conventional spare
Transmission, AOD-E with police calibration
Transmission oil cooler, external, front-mounted
Voltage regulator, electronic
Wheels, heavy-duty steel, 15 x 6.5-in.

Available Options

Auxiliary fuse panel
three ignition leads (3 connectors, 20 amp fuse)
three direct leads (3 connectors, 20 amp fuse)
Noise Suppression Package (RFI) police radio
Roof reinforcement for roof-mounted signal equipment, extra bow with center plate to header
Spotlight (left and/or right) pillar-mounted with 6-in. clear halogen bulb
Spotlight Prep Package (left and/or right)
VASCAR speedometer cable
Wiring Prep Package (required for dealer-installed spotlight)
Front and rear wiring packages and roof wiring (wires, color-coded)

Engine 4 6L V-8 SOHC

Displacement: 281 cubic inches
Sequential multi-port electronic fuel injection
EEC-IV electric engine controls
Nominal compression ratio: 9.0:1
Cast-in-block accessory mounting brackets
Hydraulic timing chain tensioner
Interchangeable aluminum cylinder heads
Roller cam followers

Horsepower and Torque Ratings

Horsepower: 210 net @ 4600 rpm
Torque: 270 lb.-ft. net @ 3400 rpm

Transmission

4-speed automatic
Electronic shift control
4th gear overdrive
4th gear lockout (in overdrive selector position)
Low-gear lockout - computerized logic prevents over-revving of the engine in low gear.

Chassis

Body-on-frame perimeter construction
Police suspension: independent SLA coil spring design with ball joints and front stabilizer bar, 1:1 ratio
Coil springs
Gas-pressurized hydraulic front shock absorbers, double-acting, vertical mount
Gas-pressurized hydraulic rear shock absorbers, double-acting, angle mount
Speed-sensitive steering, variable assist, parallelogram, front steer with center link.
Ball and nut recirculating gears
Overall gear ratio: 16.4:1
Four-bar link rear suspension with stabilizer bar

Wheelbase:		114.4"
Overall Length:		212.4"
Overall height:		56.8"
Overall width:		77.8"
Tread:	Front:	62.8"
	Rear:	63.3"
Base model curb weight		3.776 lbs.
Fuel tank capacity		20 gals.

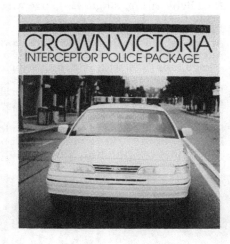

1968 Plymouth Police Cars

Fury Pursuit

Fury is the full-size model in Plymouth's 1968 lineup. The Pursuit's optional 440 cu. in. Super Commando V-8 comes equipped with a high-performance cam, 4-bbl. carb, and dual exhausts, and puts out 375 hp at 4600 rpm.

The Pursuit has optional 437.1 sq. in. brakes.

The Pursuit is equipped with a special high-speed handling package including an anti-sway bar, heavy-duty ball joint suspension, and heavy-duty shocks.

Fury Patroller

The '68 Fury Patroller is built with three things in mind: economy, endurance, and comfort.

The standard Patroller engine is Plymouth's rugged 225 cu. in. Six.

Belvedere Pursuit

For 1968, the Belvedere models are built on a 116 inch wheelbase.

The Belvedere Pursuit is equipped with a special suspension package. It includes front torsion bars and extra-heavy-duty rear leaf springs, a heavy-duty anti-sway bar, and every Belvedere Pursuit rests squarely on heavy-duty shock absorbers. The standard Belvedere Pursuit power plant turns on the speed quickly. It's a 318 cu. in V-8. Optional: our 330 hp Super Commando 383 cu. in. V-8.

Belvedere Patroller

Standard Belvedere Patroller equipment includes a 225 cu. in. Six.

A 116 in. wheelbase and heavy-duty front torsion bars combine for ideal handling and maneauverability on city streets.

Fury Police Optional Equipment

Air Cleaner: oil bath (Avail. 225 & 318 cu. in. engines only).

Fast idle throttle control, manual.

Alternators: 60 amp H.D. Chrysler 65 amp H.D. Leece Neville with dual belt drive and transistor regulator (N.A. with power steering or air cond. on 6-cyl.) (N.A. with ATC air cond. on 318 V-8). Note: All alternators have built-in silicon rectifiers.

Brakes, disc front (V-8 only) (pwr. brakes mandatory).

Roof light wiring: single 12-gauge wire. Less hole.

High-capacity fan: 7 blade; 7 blade with slip drive for 383 and 440 cu. in. engines only.

Spotlight: 5 in. left and/or right, fender-mounted remote control.

Deck lid remote release (control on instrument panel).

Engines: 383 cu. in. Commando 2-bbl. V-8, 383 cu. in. Super Commando 4-bbl. V-8 (w/Torque-Flite only), 440 cu. in. Commando 4-bbl. V-8 (w/TorqueFlite only), 440 cu. in. Super Commando 4-bbl. V-8 (N.A. wagons; w/TorqueFlite only).

Belvedere Police Optional Equipment

Air Cleaner: oil bath (Avail. 225 & 318 cu. in. engines only).

Roof light wiring: single 12-gauge wire, less hole.

Trim: heavy-duty all-vinyl tan, coupe and sedan only.

Radio suppression package.

Armrests: rear with ash receivers, coupe only.

Alternators: 60 amp H.D. Chrysler 65 amp H.D. Leece Neville with dual belt drive and transistor regulator (N.A. with power steering or air cond. on 6-cyl.) Note: All alternators have built-in silicon rectifiers.

Brakes, disc front (V-8 only) (pwr. brakes mandatory).

Deck lid remote release (control on instrument panel).

Fast idle throttle control, manual.

Spotlight: 5 in. left and/or right, fender-mounted remote control.

Engines: 383 cu. in Commando 2-bbl. V-8 (N.A. 3-spd. man. trans.), 383 cu. in. Super Commando 4-bbl. V-8 (N.A. 3-spd. man. trans.).

1977 Plymouth Police Cars

For 1977, you can order the big 440-cubic-inch, 4-barrel, heavy-duty V-8 with dual exhausts and dual catalytic converters for your Fury Police Pursuit - and you also get the Electronic Lean-Burn system automatically in all counties outside California where altitude is under 4,000 feet.

A 400-cubic-inch, 4-barrel heavy-duty V-8 with Electronic Lean-Burn system is also available on the Fury Police Pursuit. This single-exhaust engine is not available in California or at altitude above 4,000 feet.

Features of the 440 and 400 heavy-duty V-8s include:

Double-roller timing chain drive between the crankshaft and camshaft designed for durability.

Hot-pressed valve springs are engineered for better performance than ordinary valve springs.

Chrome-flashed exhaust valve stems have hardened tips

Moly-filled top rings have excellent scuff resistance to protect both the rings and the cylinder walls

Anti-turbulence windage tray between the crankshaft and oil pump reduces turbulence and improves performance

Crankshaft of shot-peened nodular cast iron

Electronic spark advance and electronic ignition.

Features of the Fury Pursuit Model

High-capacity alternator designed and manufactured by Chrysler Corporation rated at 100 amperes

A 500-ampere (85-ampere-hour) Long-life battery with thermo-guard heat shield

A modular instrument panel construction allows quick, easy service operations to be performed from the passenger side of the panel

Features of the Gran Fury Pursuit Model

Standard tires for Gran Fury Police Pursuits are special "70" series wide fabric-belted radial-ply high-performance blackwall tires. They are designed to meet the police need for better handling high-performance tires with good wet traction and long tread life.

A special handling package is provided with specific suspension for pursuit-type work. The package contains the following specially matched heavy-duty components for high-speed operation: front and rear sway bar, heavy-duty torsion bars, heavy-duty rear leaf springs with anti-brake-hop clamps, extended-life upper and lower control-arm bushings, and large heavy-duty front and rear shock absorbers -- 1-3\16-in. front and 1-3\8-in. rear.

Heavy-duty police-type brakes are used on all models. They are power disc in the front with semi-metallic pads, and 11 x 2.5-in. drum-type automatic adjusting brakes in the rear. A large-capacity dual-tandem, diaphragm-type power booster and dual master brake cylinder are standard.

The power steering for police is a special unit with selected gears for minimum free play, and a special high-rate internal spring to provide a firm feel. A cooler for the power steering oil is standard. A three-spoke steering wheel with partial horn ring is standard on police models.

Features of the 440 and 400 heavy-duty V-8 engines:

Aluminum-alloy main bearings and tri-metal connecting-rod bearings provide greater durability and high temperature protection.

High-load valve springs with dampers on the 440 minimize valve float to provide engine durability and power at high speeds.

A windage tray between the crankshaft and oil sump increases power by decrasing turbulence.

Exhaust valve stems are chromed and have hardened tips for increased resistance to wear.

Double-roller timing chain drive between the crankshaft and camshaft is designed for greater durability.

Dual catalytic converters, on the 440 only, combine with the 440's dual exhaust to minimize back pressure.

Rear spark plugs are protected by double-walled heat shields.

The crankshaft is shot-peened nodular cast iron.

Exhaust manifolds are of a thick-wall construction to improve endurance.

Moly-filled top compression rings have excellent scuff resistance to protect both the rings and the cylinder walls.

100 percent silicone-insulated ignition wiring is used because it withstands high operating temperatures.

Fury   Gran Fury

Standard Equipment

Air Cleaner - Dry-type replaceable element unsilenced
Alternator - 100-ampere heavy-duty Chrysler with heavy-duty transistorized regulator
+m-65-ampere heavy-duty Chrysler
Ammeter - 100-ampere
Antifreeze for minus 35 degrees F
Armrests, front and rear
Ash Receivers, rear
Axle Ratio - 3.21
Battery - 500 ampere (85 ampere-hours) with Thermo-Guard heat shield
Brakes - Dual master cylinder all models Heavy-duty Police-type semi-metallic, disc front, drum rear, automatic-adjusting (Includes dual tandem booster on Fury and Gran Fury -- except Fury wagons)
Coolant Recovery System
Cooling - Max. capacity radiator, 7-blade fan and fan shroud. Flex-type fan or thermal torque-drive fan
Electronic Ignition System
Engine Mount - Spool type
Gauge - Oil pressure
Grass Shield for catalytic converter
Heater with Defroster
Horns - Dual
Horn Ring - Partial
Inside Hood Release
Interiors, Gran Fury - Heavy-duty cloth-and-vinyl trim in blue or black
Interiors, Fury - Heavy-duty cloth-and-vinyl trim in blue or black
Mat - Heavy-duty, black rubber, front and rear
Mirrors - Inside Day/Nite
Outside left, manual, door mounted
Oil Filter - Full-flow throw-away
Parking Brake Warning Light
Power Steering, firm-type Police
Power Steering Pump Cooler (8-cylinder only) with power steering
Seat-Back, Front-Full foam
Seat Belts - 3 front and 3 rear, with integral belts front, outboard left and right

Seat Cushion, Front - Heavy-duty
Special Handling Package - Designed and engineered for pursuit-type work. Includes heavy-duty front and rear sway bar (except wagons), torsion bars, heavy-duty rear springs, and heavy-duty shock absorbers
Structural Reinforcement and additional welds
Suspension, Heavy-Duty - Includes front sway bar, torsion bars, heavy-duty rear springs and heavy-duty shock absorbers
Above suspension with rear sway bar
(V-8 only)
Special Heat Reflective Rubber Splash Shield, right side
Speedometer - Certified calibrated 120 mph
Speedometer - Certified calibrated 140 mph
Stop Light Switch - Heavy-duty
Thermostatic Ignition Control Valve, V-8 engines (except 318 and 400 V-8s in all counties under 4,000 feet except California)
Transmission, Auxiliary Oil Cooler
Transmission - Automatic TorqueFlite, 3-speed
Windshield Wipers - 2-speed and electric washers

Fury   *Gran Fury*

Optional Equipment
Air Conditioning
Alternator, 100-Ampere (8-cylinder models)
Deck Lid - Remote Release, Electric (Control on instrument panel)
Defroster - Rear window - electric heated
Defroster - Rear window - blower type
Differential - Sure-Grip, 3.21 or 2.71
3.21 only
Engine Oil Cooler (with E58, E68 and E86 V-8 engines only)
Fast-Idle Throttle Control - Manual locking type
Floor Pan Sound Insulation (Same as standard Fury V-8)
Gauge - Oil and temperature assembly (Not available with clock)
Hood Release, Inside
Keys - Single - Same key for all locks on car, different key for each car
Keys - Universal single system - Same key for all locks on cars, same key for all cars in fleet
Locking Gas Cap
Mirror - Right outside, manual (to match left remote-control mirror style)
Mirror - Right outside, remote. (Available only in combination with left remote outside mirror)
Mirror - Inside, day-nite
Parking Brake Release, Automatic
Power Steering, Police firm type
Radio Cable Conduit (1-5\8-in. diameter)
Radio Suppression Package
Roof Reinforcement Plate
Seat - Heavy-duty rear including foam cushions (with heavy-duty vinyl trim only on Fury)
Spotlight, white bulb #4435
A-pillar mounted 6" left
A-pillar mounted 6" right
Stainless-Steel Hose Clamps - Screw-type
Tinted Glass - All windows
Trim, Gran Fury Heavy-duty all-vinyl in gold or black
Fury - Heavy-duty vinyl in gold, blue or black
Volare - Heavy-duty vinyl in black, blue or parchment
Heavy-Duty Floor Mats, black only (Standard on Police models)
Steering Wheel with partial horn ring, black only (Standard on Police models)
Engine Availability - Police Models and Packages - Federal Emissions Package (Under 4,000-ft. Altitude). All engines for police service have catalytic converters and require unleaded fuel.

1977 Plymouth Police Cars

Engine - Cubic-inch - Carburetor	Net Torque	Net Horsepower	Fury	Gran Fury
225 Six 1-bbl. H.D.	170 @ 1600 RPM	100 @ 3600 RPM	X	NA
318 V-8 2-bbl. H.D.	245 @ 1600 RPM	145 @ 4000 RPM	X	NA
360 V-8 2 bbl. H.D.	275 @ 2000 RPM	155 @ 3600 RPM	X	X

Engine - Cubic-inch - Carburetor	Net Torque	Net Horsepower	Fury	Gran Fury
360 V-8 4-bbl. H.D.	275 @ 2000 RPM	175 @ 4000 RPM	NA	NA
400 V-8 4-bbl. H.D.	305 @ 3200 RPM	190 @ 3600 RPM	X	X
440 V-8 4-bbl.	320 @ 2000 RPM	195 @ 3600 RPM	NA	X
440 V-8 4-bbl. Dual Exhaust, Dual Catalytic Converter H.D.	350 @ 3200 RPM	245 @ 4000 RPM	X	X

1982 PLYMOUTH GRAN FURY POLICE CAR EQUIPMENT

Standard Equipment (With A38 Pursuit Package)

Air Cleaner - Dry type, replaceable element

Alternator - Heavy-duty SAE 114-ampere Chrysler alternator with transistorized regulator (dual-belt drive for V-8s; single-belt for six-cyl)

Antifreeze - For minus 35 degrees F protection with highter boiling point

Armrests - Front and rear

Ash Receiver - Front

Ash Receiver - Rear; two, in armrests

Automatic Air Conditioning Compressor High-Pressure Clutch Cutoff Switch - With optional air conditioning

Axle Ratio - Rear: 2.9:1

Axle Size - Rear: 8.25-in. diameter ring gear

Battery - 500-ampere Long-Life (maintenance-free), with heat shield (120-minute reserve capacity)

Battery Feed Wire (8-gauge) for Police Accessories - From battery to passenger compartment through grommet in firewall; includes two jumper wires and fusible-link protection

Body - Reinforced forestructure and additional welding

Body - Reinforced rear structure and additional welding

Brakes - Heavy-duty power brakes with dual master cylinder for separate front and rear braking systems: disc front brakes with semi-metallic pads: 11 x 2.5-in. rear drum brakes with automatic adjusters

Brakes, Power Booster - Single diaphragm

Carpet, Floor - Color-keyed

Catalytic Converter

Catalytic Converter Grass Shield - For optional V-8s

Coolant Recovery System

Electronic Ignition

Engine - 3.7-liter (225 cu. in.) 1-bbl Slant Six

Engine Cooling Package - Maximum capacity radiators: 22-in. width radiator with 6-cyl engine, 26-in. width radiator with V-8 engines; thermal torque drive cooling fans: 18-in. diameter fan with 6-cyl engine, 20-in. diameter fan with V-8s

Engine Mounts - Spool type

Fuel Tank - 18 gals.

Gauges - Engine temperature, ammeter, fuel (oil pressure gauge available: limited production)

Glass, Tinted - All windows (includes shaded windshield)

Heater with Defroster

Hood Release, Inside - Instrument-panel mounted

Horns - Dual

Hubcaps - Vented

Ignition - Electronic, Chrysler System

Mirrors - Inside day/night, windshield-mounted

Outside left, manual

Oil Filler Tube - Easy-fill: with optional V-8s only

Oil Filter - Full-flow, throwaway

Oil Pressure Warning Light

Parking Brake Warning Light
Radio - AM (delete radio option available)
Seat, Front - Heavy-duty cushion with full-foam seatback
Seat Belts - Three front, three rear (driver and right front passenger seats have combined lap-shoulder belts)
Shock Absorbers, Heavy-Duty - Front and rear: 1-3\16-in.
Speedometer - Noncertified, 85 mph
Steering, Power - Special Pursuit Firm-Feel type (oil cooler included with optional V-8 engines)
Stoplight Switch - Heavy-duty (regular-duty switch with optional automatic speed control)
Suspension - Specially designed and engineered suspension for pursuit-type work; includes front and rear antisway bars, heavy-duty rear leaf springs with special bushings, heavy-duty strut bearings and heavy-duty front and rear shock absorbers
Transmission, Automatic TorqueFlite - 3-speed, column-mounted range selector, with auxiliary transmission oil cooler
Transmission Low-Gear Blockout
Voltage Regulator - Electronic, Chrysler
Wheels - Extra-heavy-duty: 15 x 7.0
Windshield Washer - Electric
Windshield Wipers - Two-speed electric with washers

Optional Equipment (With A38 Pursuit Package)
Air Conditioning
Deck Lid Release, Remote - Electric: control on instrument panel
Defroster, Rear Window - Electrically heated
Dome Light Door Switch Control Deactivation
Engine Block Heater
Engine Oil Cooler - Available V-8s only
Hose Clamps - Stainless steel, screw type
Keys, Single - Same key for all locks on car, different key for each car (not available with optional tilt steering column)
Keys, Universal - Same key for all locks on all 1982 cars in fleet (not available with optional tilt steering column)
Lamp, Glove Box
Lamp, Luggage Compartment
Lamp, Underhood
Light, Additional Dome
Mats, Floor - Heavy-duty: black only (available with A3, F4, KX, K2 trims only)
Mirror, Outside Right - Remote control
Oil Pressure Gauge
Police Bonding Strap Package - Includes braided bonding straps as follows: exhaust system, four straps; hood-to-body, two straps; deck lid-to-body, one strap; transmission-to-chassis, one strap; engine-to-chassis, one strap; engine-to-body, one strap
Radiator and Heater Hoses, Silicon - Requires optional F83 stainless steel hose clamps (available only with optional V-8 engines and optional air conditioning)
Radio Communication Cable Conduit
Radio Delete Option
Radio Suppression Package - Standard, with radio
Rear Axle, Sure-Grip - 2.9:1 ratio
Relay Control System, Police - Includes one #10-gauge direct battery feed wire with 30-ampere circuit breaker; two #12 wire circuits with ignition key control (through relay) with 20-ampere circuit breakers on each; and two #10 ground wires (F45 battery feed wire required)
Roof, Reinforcement Plate - For light or siren
Roof Wire - Six 12-gauge and two 16-gauge wires with roof hole on roof centerline, 19 in. to the rear of the windshield
Roof Wire - Six 12-gauge and two 16-gauge wires with roof hole on right side of roof near center pillar
Roof Wire - Six 12-gauge and two 16-gauge wires without roof hole
Seat, Rear, Heavy-Duty - Full-foam cushion
Spare Tire, Compact - No-cost option (not available with D91 Sure-Grip axle)
Speedometer, Certified - Calibrated to 125 mph: includes oil pressure warning light
Spotlight, Left, 6" - Windshield-pillar-mounted
Spotlight, Right, 6" - Windshield-pillar-mounted
Throttle Control, Fast Idle - Manual locking type
Wheel Covers - Vented: 15-in.

1982 Plymouth Police Car Engines

Gran Fury Pursuit Engines
The 3.7-liter (225 cu. in.) one-barrel heavy-duty Slant Six police engine is standard on Gran Fury Pursuit. This engine has a heavy-duty exhaust manifold. Also molybdenum filled top rings for oil economy at high mileage. Hydraulic valve lifters provide quiet operation and reduce maintenance.

The 5.2-liter (318 cu. in.) two-barrel Heavy-duty V-8 police engine is optional on Gran Fury Pursuit. This engine has the following features:

Double roller timing chain
High-temperature valve seals and shields
The 5.2-liter (318 cu. in.) four-barrel heavy-duty V-8 police engine is optional on Gray Fury Pursuit. This engine has the following features:
Anti-turbulence windage tray between crankshaft and oil sump
Chrome-plated top piston rings
Crankshaft made of select hardness cast nodular iron
Detonation sensor
Double roller timing chain
Easy-access oil filler
Forged steel connecting rods
Heavy-duty chrome-plate oil rings
Heavy-duty exhaust manifolds
Heavy-duty valve springs
High-strength rocker arms
High-temperature valve seals and shields
High-temperature cylinder head ocver gaskets
Lubrite-treated camshaft
Nimonic exhaust valves
Special Kolene-cleaned cylinder heads
Special piston-to-block clearances
Special silichrome-1 high-temperature steel intake valves
Water pump with oversize bearing

Torque and Horsepower Ratings - Plymouth Police Car Engines

Engine Displacement and Carburetor	Availability	Net Torque (lb.-ft)	Net Horsepower
3.7-liter (225 CID) 1-bbl Slant Six	Gran Fury	160 @ 1,600 rpm	90 @ 3,600 rpm
5.2-liter (318 CID) 2-bbl V-8	Gran Fury	230 @ 2,000 rpm	130 @ 4,000 rpm
5.2-liter (318 CID) 4-bbl V-8	Gran Fury	240 @ 2,000 rpm	165 @ 4,000 rpm

1969 Dodge Police Vehicles

Polara Coronet

Standard Equipment
Air Cleaner - Dry-type replaceable element - unsilenced
Alternator - 46-ampere H.D. Chrysler
Ammeter - 60-ampere
Axle Ratio:
6-cyl. man. trans. 3.55, opt. 3.23
6-cyl. TorqueFlite 3.23, opt. 2.94, 3.55
8-cyl. man. trans. 3.23, opt. 3.55
8-cyl. TorqueFlite 3.23, opt. 2.94, 3.55
8-cyl. man. trans. or TorqueFlite 3.23
Battery - 70-amp-hour with battery heat shield
Brakes - dual master cylinder all models H.D., 11 x 3-in. front, 11 x 2.5-in. rear, manual-adjusting, special police lining
H.D., 11 x 3-in. front, 11 x 3-in. rear, manual-adjusting

Clutch - H.D., 11-in. on 6-cyl., 10-1\2-in. on 8-cyl.
Cleaner Air System
Cooling:
Fan shroud & hood to radiator seals
High-capacity radiator and fan shroud on all 8-cylinder models
Electrical Safety Link in Charging Circuit
Hazard Warning System
Heater - Fresh-air w/defrosters
Horns - Dual
Interiors:
H.D. cloth and vinyl trim (Tan) or standard Coronet Deluxe trim on sedans
H.D. cloth and vinyl trim (Gray) or standard Polara trims
Coronet wagon, all-vinyl trim same as standard Coronet wagon
Padded sun visors - right and left
Mat - H.D., black rubber, front and rear
Mirrors:
Interior rear-view, day/night, Outside left
Oil Filter - Full-flow: Replacement element on 225 and 318, Throw-away type on 383 or 440
Reinforcement-Roof for siren and/or flasher unit
H.D. seat and seat-back springs
front and rear (front seat only on Coronet Coupe and Wagon)
Front seat-back surface supported by hardboard backing
Seat Belts - 3-front and 3-rear
Shoulder Belts-front, left and right
Side Marker Reflectors
Special Police Handling Package-standard on all Polaras and on Coronet V-8 sedans and coupes
Includes heavy-duty sway bar, heavy-duty torsion bars, extra-heavy-duty rear springs with corrosion-resistant zinc inter-leaves, and heavy-duty shock absorbers.
Speedometer:
Certified calibrated
120 m.p.h.
140 m.p.h.
Steering Column:
Impact-absorbing type, heavy-duty steering shaft coupling (manual steering only)
Suspension:
Heavy-duty Police for 6 and V-8 Coronet wagons
Includes a sway bar, heavy-duty torsion bars, and heavy-duty rear springs, heavy-duty shock absorbers.
Coronet sedans and coupes, set of five 7.35x14-in. blackwall
(7.75x14-in. mandatory 383 V-8) Coronet wagons, set of five 8.25x14-in. blackwall
14 x 5.5JK extra-width wheels on sedans, coupes and wagons
Polara, set of five 8.25x15-in. blackwall
15 x 6JJ extra-width wheels
NOTE: Where cars are consitently operated at high speed, high-performance police tires are recommended. (See Optional Equipment)
Transmissions:
H.D. Manual, 3-speed column shift (N.A. on Coronet with 383 engine, and Polara with 383 4-bbl. and 440 Engines)
Windshield Wipers:
2-speed and windshield washers

Optional Equipment
Air Cleaner:
Oil-bath, 6-cyl. and 318 engines only
Air Conditioning
Alternators:
60-ampere Chrysler w/transistor regulator
65-ampere, 7020 series w/5013 transistor regulator Leece-Neville with dual belt drive (N.A. w/ power steering or A.C. on 6-cyl.)
Brakes:
Front Disc Brakes with drum-type rear self-adjusting, power brakes mandatory
Power Brakes
Differential:
Sure-Grip, 3.23 ratio only
Fans:
High capacity: 7 blades
High capacity with slip fan drive, 7 blades, with 383 or 440 engines only
Fast-idle Throttle Control, hand-operated
Keys - Single, same key for all locks on car. Different key for each car. (N.A. Power Tailgate Window on Coronet)
Keys - Universal-single, same key for all locks on car. Same key for all cars in fleet. (N.A. power tailgate window on Coronet)
Interior Trim - Heavy-duty all-vinyl (Gray on Polara, Tan on Coronet; sedans and coupes only)
Maximum Capacity Cooling Package - Less fan

Oil Gauge (N.A. with clock)
Power Steering
Radio Suppression Package
Roof Light Wiring Single, 12-gauge wire (less hole)
Spotlights
5 or 6-in. left A-post. mtd., 5 or 6-in. right A-post. mtd.
Tinted Glass
Coronet
7.75x14-in. blackwall
8.25x14-in. blackwall
7.75x15-in. blackwall (15 x 6JJ wheels)
8.25x15-in. blackwall (15 x 6JJ wheels)
8.55x15-in. Wagon only
Polara
8.55x15-in. blackwall (15 x 6JJ wheels)
8.25x15-in. blackwall (15 x 6JJ wheels)
(N.A. 440 w/A.C.)

Recommended for high-speed operation and available by special order are the following:
Coronet
8.25x15-in. blackwall Police High Performance, 15 x 6JJ wheels
Transmission
Police TorqueFlite 3-speed automatic

1969 DODGE POLICE PURSUITS

Dodge Polara Basic Specifications And Dimensions

Engine	Std	Opt	Opt	Opt	Opt
Type	V-8	V-8	V-8	V-8	V-8
Displacement (cu. in.)	318	383	383	440	440
Horsepower	230	290	330	360	375
Torque (lb.-ft.)	340	390	425	480	480
Carburetion	2-bbl.	2-bbl.	4-bbl.	4-bbl.	4-bbl.
Compression Ratio	9.2:1	9.2:1	10.0:1	10.0:1	10.1:1
Exhaust	Single	Single	Dual	Dual	Dual
Fuel	Reg	Reg	Prem	Prem	Prem

Dodge Coronet Specifications And Dimensions

Engine	Std	Opt	Opt	Opt
Type	Slant 6	V-8	V-8	V-8
Displacement (cu. in.)	225	318	383	383
Horsepower	145	230	290	330
Torque (lb.-ft.)	215	340	2-bbl.	425
Carburetion	1-bbl.	2-bbl.	2-bbl.	4-bbl.
Compression Ratio	8.4:1	9.2:1	9.2:1	10.0:1
Exhaust	Single	Single	Single	Dual
Fuel	Regular	Regular	Regular	Premium

1972 Dodge Police Fleet

Polara Coronet

Standard equipment

Air-Cleaner - Dry-type replaceable element
Alternator - 60-ampere H.D. Chrysler w/transistorized regulator
50-ampere H.D. Chrysler w/transistorized regulator
Ammeter - 80-ampere
Axle Ratio 3.23
Battery - 70-amp-hour with heat shield
Brakes - Dual master cylinder all models H.D. Police type, 11 x 3-in. front, 11 x 2.5-in. rear,
   auto. adj.
Cleaner Air System
Cooling - High-capacity radiator. 7-blade fan and fan shroud on V-8s. Torque drive fan std. on
   400 and 440 V-8s
Electrical Safety Link in Charging circuit
Engines - 225 cu.in., 6-cyl., single 1-bbl., 8.4:1 comp. ratio, regular fuel
318-cu.-in., V-8, single 2-bbl., 8.6:1 comp. ratio, regular fuel
Engine Mount Restraint on 225, 318, and 360 engines
Evaporative Emission Control System
Hazard Warning System
Head Restraints - left and right
Heater - Fresh-air w/defrosters
Horns - Dual
Inside Hood Release
Interiors - H.D. cloth and vinyl (Tan) or std. Coronet trim on sedans
H.D. cloth and vinyl from (Gray) or special cloth and vinyl trims in blue, tan or black
Mat - H.D., black rubber, front and rear
Mirrors - Inside glareproof
Outside left, door mounted
Oil Filter - Full-flow throw-away
Padded Sun Visors - Right and left
Parking Brake Warning Light
Power Steering
Rear Crossmember Reinforcement
Reinforcement, Roof - For siren and/or light
Seats - Foam seat cushion - front and rear
Seat and Seat-back springs, heavy-duty - front and rear
Front seat-back surface supported by hardboard backing
Seat Belts - 3 front and 3 rear
Shoulder Belts - Front left and right
Special Handling Package - Designed and engineered for pursuit-type work - standard on all
   Polaras - Includes heavy-duty sway bar, heavy-duty torsion bars, extra-heavy-duty rear
   springs and heavy-duty shock absorbers (1-3\16-in. front and 1-3\8-in. rear for Polara)
Speedometer - Certified calibrated 120 m.p.h. on Coronet, 140 m.p.h. on Polara
Steering, H.D. - Shaft coupling - Manual steering only
Steering column - Energy-absorbing type with ignition lock
Suspension - Heavy-duty for all Coronet sedans. All heavy-duty components for police patrol work.
   Includes torsion bars, heavy-duty rear springs, heavy-duty one-inch shock absorbers front and
   rear. Sway bar is special equipment on 6-cyl. sedan (Rear sway bar is std. w/400 4-bbl. and 440
   4-bbl.)
Tires - Coronet sedans, set of five E78x14-in. blackwall 225 and 318, F78x14-in. with 400 and
   440, and 318 w/air conditioning
14 x 5.5JJ extra-width wheels
Polara set of five (F78x15-in. with 318, 360, G78 with 400 2-bbl. and 440 4-bbl., and with all
   engines with air conditioning
15 x 6JJ extra-width wheels
Transmission - H.D., automatic
Windshield Wipers - 2-speed and washers

Polara Coronet

Optional equipment

Air Conditioning
Alternators - 60-amperes Chrysler w/transistorized regulator
65-ampere, 7020 seriesw/5013 transistor regulator, Leece-Neville heavy-duty with dual belt
   drive (N.A. w/power steering, A.C., or Calif. emission package on 6-cyl.) (N.A. w/power steering and Calif. emission pkg. on 400 and 440 engines)
NOTE: 85 or 105 Amp. Leece-Neville available by special order
Brakes - H.D. Police Front Disc Brakes with semi-metallic disc lining, drum type rear, 11 x 2.5-
   in. Automatic adjusting, power brakes mandatory
Bucket Seats (all vinyl or cloth and vinyl)

Differential - Sure-Grip, 3.23
Engines - 360 cu.-in. V-8, single 2-bbl., 8.0:1 comp. ratio regular fuel
400 cu.-in. V-8, 4-bbl., 8.2:1 comp. ratio, single exhaust regular fuel
440 cu.-in. V-8, 4-bbl., Magnum 8.2:1 comp. ratio, dual exhaust regular fuel
Fans - High-capacity, 7-blades, Std. 8-cyl.
High capacity with slip fan drive, 7 blades with 400 or 440 engines only
Fast-Idle Throttle Control - Manual locking type
Gauge, Oil Pressure
Keys - Single - Same key for all locks on car, different key for each car
Keys - Universal 2-key system - Same key for all locks on cars, same keys for all cars in fleet
Interior Trim - Heavy-duty, all-vinyl (Gray on Polara, Tan or Black on Coronet)
Locking Gas Cap
Maximum Capacity Cooling Package - Less fan
Oil Filter - Replaceable Element (225 and 318 only)
Power Steering (Manual steering available on Polara)
Radio Suppression Package
Roof Light Wiring - Single, 12-gauge wire (less hole)
Spotlights - 5 or 6-in. right "A" pillar mounted
5 or 6-in. left "A" pillar mounted
Tinted Glass - Windshield only
All Windows
Tires - High Performance Police Type (set of five) 4-ply, polyester bias construction with 2 fiberglass
    belts. Strongly recommended for high-speed service. G78x15-in. blackwall. H78x15-in. blackwall

1972 DODGE POLICE FLEET

Dodge Polara Basic Dimensions

Engine	Std	Opt	Opt	Opt	Opt	Opt.
Type	V-8	V-8	V-8	V-8	V-8	V-8
Displacement (cu. in.)	318	360	400	400	440	440
Carburetion	2-bbl	2-bbl	2-bbl	4-bbl	4-bbl	4-bbl
Compression Ratio	8.6:1	8.8:1	8.2:1	8.2:1	8.2:1	8.2:1
Exhaust	Single	Single	Single	Dual	Dual	Dual
Fuel	Reg	Reg	Reg	Reg	Reg	Reg

Dodge Coronet

Engine	Std	Std	Opt	Opt	Opt
Type	Slant 6	V-8	V-8	V-8	V-8
Displacement (cu. in.)	225	318	400	400	440
Carburetion	1-bbl.	2-bbl.	2-bbl.	4-bbl.	4-bbl.
Compression Ratio	8.4:1	8.6:1	8.2:1	8.2:1	8.2:1
Exhaust	Single	Single	Single	Dual	Dual
Fuel	Reg	Reg	Reg	Reg	Reg

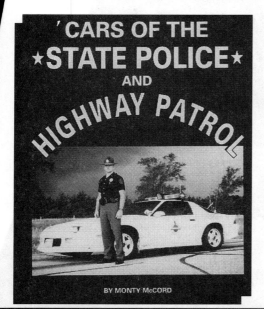
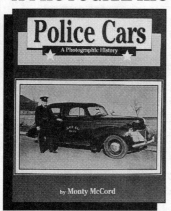

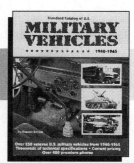